Practical Chinese Reader II

Patterns and Exercises

New and Revised
Simplified Character Edition

Cheng & Tsui Company

实用汉语课本

Practical Chinese Reader II
Patterns and Exercises

New and Revised

Simplified Character Edition

汉字作业簿

简体字本

陈 凌 霞
Ling-hsia Yeh

Cheng & Tsui Company

About the Author

Ling-hsia Yeh is an assistant professor of Chinese in the Department of Asian Languages and Literatures, University of Massachusetts, Amherst. She received her B.A. degree in Foreign Languages and Literatures from National Taiwan University, and her M.A. and Ph.D. degrees in linguistics from Indiana University.

Cheng & Tsui Company
25 West Street
Boston, MA 02111-1213 USA
e-mail orders@cheng-tsui.com

New and Revised Simplified Character Edition 0-88727-208-8
New and Revised Traditional Character Edition 0-88727-200-2

Companion textbook, writing workbooks, computer software, video tapes and audio tapes are available from the publisher.

Printed in the United States of America

PUBLISHER'S NOTE

The Cheng & Tsui Company is pleased to announce the most recent volume of the *C&T Asian Language Series,* the new and revised edition of *Practical Chinese Reader II: Patterns and Exercises.* This workbook supplements the highly successful introductory Chinese language textbook *Practical Chinese Reader II,* compiled by the Beijing Language Institute.

The C&T Asian Language Series is designed to publish and widely distribute quality language texts as they are completed by teachers at leading educational institutions. *The C&T Asian Language Series* is devoted to significant works in the field of Asian languages developed in the United States and elsewhere.

We welcome readers' comments and suggestions concerning the publications in this series. Please contact the following members of the Editorial Board:

NOTE ON THE SECOND EDITION

Except for a few places where some corrections have been made, the contents of this edition are essentially the same as those of the first edition. However, the reader may find useful the three appendices which are newly added. The typing of the three appendices is supported by part of a Faculty Research Grant from the University of Massachusetts at Amherst. I am appreciative of Mr. Tong Shen and Mr. Shaodan Lo for their meticulous work of typing the draft of the appendices.

CONTENTS

Preface i
Acknowledgements ii
Abbreviations iv

Lesson 31 1
Lesson 32 8
Lesson 33 14
Lesson 34 21
Lesson 35 27
Lesson 36 31
Lesson 37 38
Lesson 38 45
Lesson 39 51
Lesson 40 58
Lesson 41 62
Lesson 42 68
Lesson 43 74
Lesson 44 80
Lesson 45 87
Lesson 46 91
Lesson 47 96
Lesson 48 101
Lesson 49 107
Lesson 50 112

Appendices

I: Chinese-Pinyin-English Index 115
II: English-Pinyin-Chinese Index 135
III: Stroke Number Index 161

PREFACE

This workbook was written with the intention of providing a companion to the textbook *Practical Chinese Reader: Book II,* compiled by the Beijing Language Institute. Although it is meant to be a sequel to *Practical Chinese Reader I: Patterns and Exercises* by Professor Madeline Chu of Kalamazoo College, Michigan, it does not entirely follow the format and approach adopted in her book.

The organization of the workbook is such that for each lesson, except review lessons, there is a grammar review followed by a set of exercises. The grammar review attempts to provide an overall presentation of the grammar and sentence patterns in every lesson. A certain portion of the exercises are designed to reflect those patterns and their usages. The students are then required to decide what to use and when to use their knowledge of the grammar in the related exercises. The grammar notes follow as closely as possible the explanations in the textbook, with the exception of lessons 39 and 47, where certain verb-type words are considered as post-verbal prepositions rather than resultative verb complements.

The goal of the exercises is to familiarize students with the vocabulary, sentence structure, and content of every lesson. There are generally four to five exercises in each lesson. The forms frequently employed include fill-in-the blanks, word-order, question and answer, sentence completion, structural change, and translation. The arrangement of the exercises for each lesson is such that practice on vocabulary comes first, followed by those on structure and content, with the translation exercises at the very end, since they require knowledge of both vocabulary and grammar.

Not many compositional exercises are included since they can always be assigned by individual instructors to serve their own needs. The compositional exercises given in this workbook are controlled ones in the sense that vocabulary and sentence structure for writing the compositions are controlled within the limit of related lessons. At the same time, students are still allowed to stretch their imaginations.

A few words must be said about some of the English sentences in the translation exercises. Although they may not sound idiomatic, those sentences are written deliberately either to correspond to the structures of their Chinese counterparts or to give clues to certain Chinese structures. This is done to avoid the possibility of coming up with misleading translations for the exercises.

The author welcomes comments and suggestions from users of this volume. This author alone is responsible for any mistakes that may be found in this book.

– Ling-hsia Yeh
University of Massachusetts, Amherst
January 1991

i

ACKNOWLEDGEMENTS

I am grateful to the Five Colleges East Asian Languages Program for providing me with a grant which made possible the completion of this work in its present form.

I should like to express my sincere appreciation to the following people for their assistance and encouragement:

> Members of the Editorial Board of the Cheng & Tsui Company's *Asian Language Series* for their comments and suggestions for revising the manuscript;

> Professor Donald Gjertson for going over the translation exercises and for polishing the sentences;

> Professor Shou-hsin Teng for his encouragement and generous loan of the Chinese computer software program used in producing this work;

> Ms. Jiaxiang Dai for typing the translation exercises.

I should like to express special thanks to Mr. Tong Shen, a Ph.D. candidate in the linguistics department of the University of Massachusetts, Amherst for typing, editing and printing the manuscript numerous times. Without his patience and meticulous work, the final draft would not have been completed in its present form.

Finally, I would like to thank my colleagues, and especially Nina Rose-Racine, of the Department of Asian Languages and Literatures for their moral support.

– Ling-hsia Yeh
University of Massachusetts, Amherst

ABBREVIATIONS

Adjective	Adj
Adverb	Adv
Aspect	Asp
Interrogative Pronoun	IP
Negation	Neg
Noun Phrase	NP
Object	Obj
Other Element	OE
Preposition	Prep
Question Device	QD
Subject	Subj
Stative Verb	SV
Verb Phrase	VP

Note: Words with asterisk following them are those given in the supplementary vocabulary lists.

Interaction between time-measure complements (TMC) and verbal -了 as well as the sentential 了

I. Regular pattern

  A. Verbs without objects

    1. Habitual or future events

      Subj (+ OE) + Verb + TMC
      他　　每天　　　学习　　两个小时。
      (He studies for two hours every day.)

    2. Past events

      Subj (+ OE) + Verb + -le + TMC
      他　　昨天　　　锻炼　　了　　一个小时。
      (He exercised for an hour yesterday.)

      王老师 在中国　　住　　　了　　三个月。
      (Professor Wang stayed in China for three months.)

    3. Events which took place in the past and have been carried into the moment of utterance

      Subj (+ OE) + verb + -le + TMC + le
      我　　已经　　　学习　　了　两个小时　了。
      (I have been studying for two hours.)

  B. Verbs with objects

    1. Habitual or future events

      Subj (+ OE) + Verb + Obj + Verb + TMC
      他　　想　　学习　　汉语　　学习　　一年。
      (He intends to study Chinese for a year.)

    2. Past events

      Subj (+ OE) + Verb + Obj + Verb + -le + TMC
      他　　在中国　　学习　　汉语　　学习　　了　　一年。
      (He studied Chinese in China for a year.)

    3. Events which took place in the past and continued to the moment of utterance

      Subj (+ OE) + Verb + Obj (+ OE) + Verb + -le + TMC + le
      他　　在中国　学习　汉语　已经　　学习　　了　　一年　了。
      (He has been studying Chinese in China for a year.)

II. Insertion pattern

This pattern applies to sentences with non-specific verbal objects and only if the objects are not pronouns.

Subj (+ OE) + Verb + (-le) + TMC + (de) + Obj + (le)
他　　想　学习　　　　　两年　的　汉语。
(He intends to study Chinese for two years.)

他　　昨天　看　　　了 一个小时 的　　电视。
(He watched television for an hour yesterday.)

我　　已经　　坐　　　了 十个小时 的　　飞机　了。
(I have been on the airplane for ten hours.)

III. The usage of 多 with a numeral

A. When the numeral is 'ten' or less

Numeral + Measure + 多 + Noun
三　　　　个　　　多　　小时

B. When the numeral is 'ten' or more

Numeral + 多 + Measure + Noun
三十　　多　　个　　　小时

C. Exceptions: 天 and 年 behave like measure words.

三年多
四天多
三十多年
二十多天

Fill in appropriate vocabulary:

1. 你在这儿住了多长（____ ____）了？
   (shi jian)
   you at here lived many long (Time)

2. 你学了 ____ 年中文了？
   ji
   you studied how many years chinese

3. 1965年我 ____ 二次回中国，参观了很多工厂。
   di   con guan   gong chong
                                     Factory

4. 北京是中国的 ____ ____ 。

5. 一天有二十四个 ____ ____ 。
   one day have 24   xiao shi
                       hours

6. 去中国以前我们先要去办 ____ ____ 。

7. 北京的机场是一个 ____ ____ 机场。

8. 中国是一个（____ ____ 主义的)国家。
   China is one Socialistic Country

9. 中国希望 ____ ____ 四个现代化。

10. 我的妈妈很 ____ ____ ，每天工作十个小时。

11. 在外国住了很久的中国人叫 ____ ____ ____ 。

12. 希望你们能 ____ 国家作(一点事)。
    Xi wong neng wei
    hope they to be able to (For) country to do (Something)

13. 我在上海住了三 ____ 多月。

3

Word order:

1. 我　　回国　　1963年　　第一次

2. 我　　住了　　在　　三个多月　　上海

3. 你家里　　在北京　　有人　　还　　吗

4. 我　三十　教书　已经　多　了　年　教了

5. 学生代表　　是　　北京　　的　　语言学院　　我

6. 坐　飞机　你们　多长　了　时间　的

7. 不错　北京　真　天气　的

8. 我弟弟　　两年　　准备　　学习　　在中国　　多

9. 有　中文系　老师　位　十　多

10. 到北京　　十分钟　　有　还　要　就　了

Complete the following sentences with phrases containing time-measure complements.

1. 我们三点钟到国际机场，现在六点半，朋友还没来，我们等他已经

    _____.

2. 他九点十分去买东西，九点五十五分开车回家．他 _____
    的东西．

3. 我的朋友今年夏天要去中国学习汉语，他想明年冬天回美国． 他
    准备在中国 _____.

4. 昨天我们早上十点坐飞机，中午十二点半到那个大城．我们 ____
    _____.

5. 我们每天上午十点十分上汉语课，十一点五分下课． 我们每天
    _____汉语课．

6. 1965年王老师开始在外语学院教书． 他现在已经 _____
    _____.

7. 我每天晚上十一点睡觉，早上七点起床． 我每天 _____
    _____.

8. 那些代表们晚上七点开始开会*，现在九点四十分． 他们 ____
    _____.

5

Translate into Chinese (using regular pattern):

1. How many hours do you work every day?

2. He lived in the capital for half a year.

3. I hope I will be able to stay in China for three months.

4. How long did that overseas Chinese visit that factory?
    More than two hours.

5. That student representative has been waiting for him for
    twenty minutes.

6. How many months has he lived in the countryside?
    More than four months.

7. They did not watch TV for the whole evening. They only
    watched for a half hour or so.

8. Are you going to use the car for a long time?
    I will use it for three days.

9. Prof. Wang has been teaching in that college for over
    thirty years.

10. I have been on the plane for more than ten hours.

I. Translate into Chinese (using insertion pattern):

1. How long have you been riding on the train?

2. They watched movies for two hours and forty minutes.

3. The students have been holding a meeting for the whole evening.

4. Twenty some teachers shopped for one and a half hours yesterday.

5. This overseas Chinese intends to study Chinese for one year and a half.

II. Translate the following dialog:

A: Haven't seen you for a long time. Where have you been?
B: I went to China for three months.
A: Was it the first time that you went to China?
B: No, it was the second time.
A: Is there anyone in your family who lives in China?
B: Yes, my older brother.

I.   The experiential aspect marker 过

  Subj (+ Neg/OE) + Verb + Asp + NP (+ QD)
  我 最近   看   过 那个电影。
  (I saw that movie recently.)

  我 没(有)   看   过 那个电影。
  (I have never seen that movie.)

  你   看   过 那个电影 吗/没有?
  (Have you ever seen that movie?)

II. Verb-过 and frequency

 A. An expression of frequency follows a verb and its aspect marker.

   Subj (+ OE) + Verb + Asp + Frequency
   我 去年 透视 过   两次。
   (I had X-ray examination twice last year.)

 B. Insertion pattern is more frequently used when a verb is followed by a general noun (i.e., a non-specific noun).

   Subj + Verb + Asp + Frequency + Obj
   我   看 过   两次   中国电影。
   (I have seen Chinese movies twice.)

 C. When the object of a verb is a pronoun or an expression of location, insertion pattern is not allowed.

   我去过他家一次。
   (I have been to his home once.)

   我弟弟见过他两次。
   (My younger brother has seen him twice.)

 D. When the object of a verb is a definite noun, it is always topicalized (i.e., placed at the beginning of a sentence) and frequency therefore follows the verb.

   那个电影我看过两遍。
   (I have seen that movie twice.)

I. Fill in blanks with appropriate vocabulary.

1. 我去大学 医__ 务__ 所 看病。
wo qu da xue *yi* *wu* *suo* *bing*
I goto College (Clinic) To See a doctor

2. 我的心脏不太好，请给我 量__ 一下血压吧!
xin *tai* *liang* *xia xue ya*
my heart not very good please give To Measure Low blood pressure
I

3. 你第一 次__ 来中国吗? 不，我 第__ 二次来.
ni de yi *ci* *lai zhg gm ma* *di* *er ci lai*
you (First) come china not I (Second) come

4. 我们去医务所 ____ ____ 身体.
wo men qu yi wu suo *jian* *cha* *shen ti*
Check up body health

5. 我没 得__ 过什么大病. 七岁的时候，得 过__ 一 次__ 肺炎.
wo mei *de* *guo shen me da bing* *7 sui de shi hou* *de* *guo* *yi* *ci* *Fei yan*
has happened illness 7 yr old when pneumonia

6. 检查身体以前，请先到那儿拿一 ____ 表.
shen ti yi *nar* *yi*

7. 那个中国电影，他已经看过两 遍__ 了.
na ge *bian*
That Chinese Movie He already Saw Twice

8. 他最近去过两 次__ 北海.
ta *zu gin lian* *ci* *bei hai*
He recently gone Two Times to bei hai

9. 那个足球队赢过三 次__，也输 过__ 三次.
na ge zu qiu dui ying guo san *ci* *ye shu* *guo* *san ci*
That Football Team to win 3 times to lose 3 times
also lost 3 times

10. 这个汉字，我写过两遍了，我要 再__ 写一 ____.
zhe ge *wo xie guo bian le* *yao zai* *yi* *bian*
This character I I want again write One more time

11. 有人说 "有志者事竟成"。 我以前也听过 ____ ____ 的话。
yi qian *guo*
I also (said)

12. 爸爸妈妈给我们 生__ 命__。 老师给我们 知__ 识__ 。
sheng *ming* *zhi* *shi*
us life us Knowledge

II. Identification.

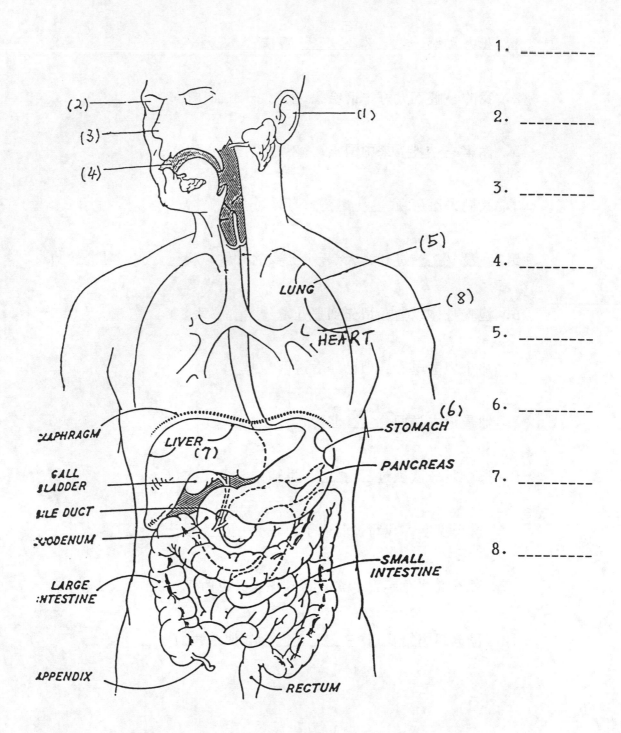

DIAPHRAGM

LIVER
(7)

GALL
BLADDER

BILE DUCT

DUODENUM

LARGE
INTESTINE

APPENDIX

(2)

(3)

(4)

(1)

(5)

LUNG

(8)

HEART

(6)

STOMACH

PANCREAS

SMALL
INTESTINE

RECTUM

1. _____

2. _____

3. _____

4. _____

5. _____

6. _____

7. _____

8. _____

Practical Chinese Reader #32 Exercise B

Fill in blanks with 了, 过 or 0 (=nothing).

X 1. 这个练习，我已经看 ____ 一遍 __了__，不会有错.

X 2. 你以前用 ____ 筷子吗？ 我没用 __过__.

X 3. 我们七点吃饭，他来 __了__ 没有？ 他还没来 ____ 呢.

X 4. 这件衬衫太小 __了__，我不想买.

X 5. 他们来 __了__ 北京一个多星期 ____，参观 ____ 很多地方.

6. 对 ____，我十岁的时候去 ____ 英国，在那儿住 ____ 三个月.

7. 你会用 ____ 毛笔写 ____ 中文吗？

8. 他看电视已经看 ____ 两个小时 ____.

9. 那本书我已经念 ____ 两遍 ____.

10. 我昨天没复习 ____ 课文，我忘 ____ 今天有汉语课.

11. 他来 ____ 找 ____ 你三次.

12. 我们就要 ____ 去 ____ 中国访问.

11

Word order:

1. 血压　一下　去　他　量　医务所

2. 电视里　中国电影　几次　我　在　看过

3. 心脏　血压　和　我的　正常　都　吗

4. 透视　到　请　一下　对面房间　吧

5. 还　我　一遍　这个电影　看　想

6. 可以　以后　透视　就　了　走

7. 要　我希望　自己　锻炼　注意　你

8. 小时候　病了　得过　我　两个月　肺炎

9. 你　拿一张表　内科　再去　先在那儿　量血压

10. 哪些地方　来北京　星期　了　你们　过　一个
    去　多

Practical Chinese Reader #32 Exercise D

Translate into Chinese:

1. Have you seen this movie before?   NI yiqian kan guo zhege dian ying ma
   No, I have never seen it.   Bu wo mei you kan guo。

2. My father has had a [shen ti] physical check-up recently.
   wo baba zui jian cha shen ti

3. Have you ever had a serious illness?
   I had pneumonia when I was ten years old.
   ni deguo de bing? wo

4. How many times have you had your blood pressure measured?

5. Have you ever seen a doctor at that infirmary?
   Yes, I have seen doctors there three times. San ci
   ni zai ge na guo c y

6. Last year his mother had an X-ray examination once.
   Ta men mama zuo nian you guo Toushi yi ci

7. I have listened to this song several times. I would like
   to listen to it once more.
   wo Ting guo zhege ger yi ge duo cl。wo yao Ting guo yi bian le

8. (How many times) have you read that (literature) book?
   ni kan guo (duo shao bian) na ben shu

9. How many times have you been to that place?
   I have been there four times.
   NI qu guo duo shao ci na ge difang? wo qu guo nar si ci

10. Please take a look at this form.
    qing, kan   zhe ge biao

11. We asked them to tell us about Beijing for a while.
    women qing Ta men (gao su) guo women yi xiar Beijing
                    (To tell)

12. I have never heard such saying before. yiqian 话
    wo yi qian you mei you ting guo zheyang de hua

13. Before you see the doctor, go to the internal medicine
    department first to get a form.

    ni kan daifu yiqian, (internal med dept)   na yi zhang biao
                      First   To get
              Xian qu

13

I. Sentential particle 了 which occurs at the end of a sentence
    may indicate a change of state.

    A. Sentences with stative verbs (or adjectival predicates)

            Subj   (+ OE) + SV + le
            天气   冷   了。
            (It is getting cold.)

            树上的叶子 都   红   了。
            (All the leaves have turned red.)

            雨   小   了.
            (The rain is letting up.)

    B. Sentences with nouns as their predicates

            现在十点了，我们回家吧。
            (It is ten o'clock. Let's go home.)

            这个孩子今年十二岁了。
            (The kid is twelve years old now.)

    C. Sentences with meteorological verbs which are always
        subjectless

            下雨了。   (It is raining.)

            刮风了。   (It is windy.)

    D. Sentences with 'verb to be', 'verb to have', modals, and
        non-adjectival type stative verbs

            现在他是大学生了。   (He is a college student now.)

            他有工作了。   (He has a job now.)

            我会说汉语了。   (I can speak Chinese now.)

II. The construction 不...了 also indicates a change of state.
     It implies that a circumstance no longer exists.

            不下雪了。   (The snow has stopped.)

14

Fill in blanks with appropriate vocabulary.

1. 有人 ____ 门，请你去开门，好吗？
   you rea   mea qing ni qu kai men hao ma

2. 春天来 了，花园里的花都 开 得很好.
   chun tian lai le   li de dou kai de hen hao
   spring comes   open

3. 这儿的冬天很冷，时间也很长，常常 刮 风，下 雪.
   zhe r de dong tian leng shi jian ye hen chang   gua   xia xue
   cold   Time   often

4. 秋天的时候，树上的 叶 子 都红 了，（大家都喜欢去看红叶.
   qiu   shu ye zi   le
   autumn Sometimes Tree   everybody

5. 张老师教我们一 首 古诗.
   jia   shŏu
   measure word

6. 梅花不 怕 冷，也不怕雪. （文学家）为 梅花写 了 不少诗.
   mei hua bu   leng   (wen xue jia) wei   mei hua xie le shai shi
   plum blossom doesn't Fear cold writer For plum To Poem
   blossom write written

7. 天气预报* 说 明天会下雪.
   tian qi yu bao shuo ming tian hai xia xue
   (Forecast) Says Tomorrow will snow

8. A. 北京的天气 ____ ____ ____ ？
   zen   me   yong
   weather how is it

   B: 不错. *not bad*
   bu cuo

9. 那儿的夏天天气很热，最热的时候到过一百 度.*
   nar de xia   xi re zue re   dao guo yi bai du
   There Summer weath very hot huttest Sometimes reaches one degrees

10. 五分钟以前还下雨，现在雨 ____ 了.
    wu fen zhong yi qian hai xia yu xian zai yu ting
    5 minutes before still raining Currently stopped

11. 今天冷吗？ 我不 ____ ____ 很冷，我觉得很暖和.
    jue de   nuan huo
    To Feel   Nice + warm

12. 那儿的天气很好，天天 都 是晴天.
    dou qing
    always clear day

Word order:

1. 公园　玩儿　今天天气　很好　你们　吗　没到

2. 有人　很热　夏天　告诉我　北京的　以前

3. 秋天　树上的　了　红　叶子　现在是　都　了

4. 梅花　大风　天气　大雪的　很好　开得　在

5. 今天　到　写了　梅花　文学家　为　不少诗
   从古时候

6. 冬天　在　有　花　什么　中国

7. 晴天　下雨　现在是　今天上午　了

8. 常常　冬天　北京的　刮风　下雪

9. 我们　时间不早　以后　谈　了　吧　再

10. 那本书　你　的　要　这是

Complete the following sentences:

1. 下雪的时候，这儿很漂亮. 你应该 _____.

2. 这儿的夏天很热，我以前不习惯，现在 _____.

3. A：他告诉我他要去检查身体.

   B：不，他有事儿，他 _____.

4. 现在是春天了. _____.

5. 秋天到了，_____.

6. 冬天来了，_____.

7. 我以前很喜欢喝咖啡，现在 _____.

8. A：你再坐一会儿.

   B：不，_____.

9. 雨停了，_____.

10. 我弟弟以前不会游泳，_____.

Translate into Chinese:

1. What time is it (now)?
   It is nine o'clock now. We shall set off pretty soon.

2. It is spring (now). All the flowers are in blossom.

3. It was raining when I came this morning. It is snowing (now).

4. It is summer (now). The weather is getting hotter.

5. Has the rain stopped?
   No, it is still very heavy.

6. He told me that he was going to have a physical check-up today.
   No, he is busy. He will not go.

7. My younger brother is a college student (now). He can drive (now).

8. I liked swimming when I was young, but I do not like it any more.

Translate into Chinese:

1. We watched football game on TV from 2:30 till 4:45.

2. A: Is it far from here to his house?

   B: Not far. It only takes ten minutes to get there.

3. A: Someone told me that winter in Beijing is long. The lowest temperature ever is ten degrees centigrade below zero.

   B: That's right. I think that spring in Beijing is best. The weather is really nice. It is neither cold nor hot. It is sunny everyday.

   A: I heard that the Summer Palace is beautiful in summer.

   B: But it is even more beautiful when there is snow.

Write a paragraph describing your reading of the cartoon.

The aspect marker 着 indicates a continued state. Possible cases employing the aspect are as follows.

A. An action verb followed by 着

> Subj   (+ Neg) + Verb + Asp (+ NP)   (+ QD)
> 他   拿   着   一封信。
> (He is holding a letter.)

> 那个女孩子   穿   着   一件红衬衫   吗/没有?
> (Does that girl wear a red blouse?)

> 营业员   没   看   着   书。
> (The clerk was not reading a book.)

B. The state of an inanimate subject

> 房间里的灯没开着。
> (The light in the room was not on.)

> 学校的门开着没有?
> (Is the gate of the school open?)

C. When a locative expression is the focus of a sentence

> Location (+ Neg) + Verb + -zhe + NP   (+ QD)
> 墙上   挂   着   一张图片。
> (A picture was hung on the wall.)

> 牌子上   没   写   着   汉字。
> (Chinese characters were not written on the sign.)

> 柜台上   放   着   邮票   没有?
> (Were stamps placed on the counter?)

D. Structures with serial verbs where 着 is attached to the first verb to form a verbal phrase describing the manner in which the second verb is performed.

> Subj (+ OE) + Verb1 + Asp (+ NP1) + Verb2 (+ NP2)
> 他们   站   着   写   信。
> (They stood while writing letters.)

> 我 喜欢 喝   着   咖啡   听   音乐。
> (I like to drink coffee while listening to music.)

21

Fill in blanks with appropriate vocabulary.

1. 这个房间的窗户前边 ＿＿＿＿ 着一张床。 床上 ＿＿＿＿ 着一本书。
   床下 ＿＿＿＿ 着一双鞋。墙上 ＿＿＿＿ 着一张画儿。画上 ＿＿＿＿ 着
   梅花。 旁边还 ＿＿＿＿ 着一首诗。

2. 外边有两个人，都 ＿＿＿＿ 着大衣。两人手里都 ＿＿＿＿ 着帽子。

3. 包裹里边装* ＿＿＿＿ 一 ＿＿＿＿ 帽子和两 ＿＿＿＿ 衬衫。

4. 他热情 ＿＿＿＿ 说："我会认真 ＿＿＿＿ 学习。"

5. 王老师笑 ＿＿＿＿ 对我说："我很高兴你能到中国去学习。"

6. 我不知道这 ＿＿＿＿ 信是谁寄的。 信封上没写 ＿＿＿＿ 寄信人的姓名。

7. 我去他家的时候，他正打 ＿＿＿＿ 电话呢！

8. 公园里边有很多人，有的坐 ＿＿＿＿ 说话，＿＿＿＿ ＿＿＿＿ 玩着球。

9. 在邮局、商店里工作的人我们叫他们 ＿＿＿＿ ＿＿＿＿ ＿＿＿＿。

10. 我想很快 ＿＿＿＿ 告诉他这个新闻，我不知道我应该 ＿＿＿＿ 信还
    是 ＿＿＿＿ 电报。

11. 我到邮局去 ＿＿＿＿ 一封信。

12. 营业员给我七 ＿＿＿＿ 邮票，二十 ＿＿＿＿ 信封。

Word order:

1. 一个　牌子　牌子上边　挂着　写着　窗口前边 字

2. 邮局里的　营业员　大声地　问　你　买什么　要

3. 要　邮局　航空信　给　朋友　去　我　寄

4. 明信片　邮票　和　柜台里边　放　很多　着

5. 姓名　地址　你的　和　下边　要写　还要

6. 医务所　一张表　拿　他　去　检查　着　身体

7. 食堂里　有的　吃饭　人很多　坐着　站着
   有的　买菜

8. 上课的时候　注意地　他　学习　下课的时候
   认真地　他　听

9. 很多电影 有的 有的 喜欢 不喜欢 看过 我 我 我

10. 图片　字　写着　没　为什么　上

Answer the following questions:

1. 你的房间住着几个人？

2. 你喜欢坐着看书还是站着看书？

3. 寄英文信的时候，寄信人的姓名和地址在信封上边还是在信封下边？

Ji ying wen xin de shi hour   Ji xin re de xing ming he di zhi zai xin Feng shan bu hai shi zai xin Feng

When mail english letter Mail letter person Full name & address envelope tup or locatim envelope

Xia bian
bottom

4. 在中国寄中文信的时候，收信人的地址在信封上边还是在信封下边？

di zhe   Xin Feng

5. 寄航空信快还是寄平信快？

6. 本市的邮局每天开几个小时？

ben shi de you Ju mei tian kai Ji ge xiao shi

MY city's post office everyday open how many hours

7. 每天上课的时候来得晚的人，以后应该怎么样？

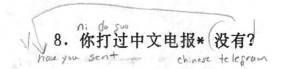

8. 你打过中文电报* 没有？

ni da guo

have you sent   chinese telegram

9. 从这儿到你家的信要多少天？

From here to your house how many days arrive

10. 你为什么学习汉语？

Translate into Chinese:

1. The clerk wore a new shirt. He was holding a postcard in
   his hand. ying ye yuan chuan (zhe) — Jian chenshan. Ta...
   着
   Ta shou li na zhe — Jeng ming xin pian

2. Was the TV in the living-room on?
   No, it wasn't on.

3. A table was placed in front of the window.

4. Many beautiful stamps were placed inside the counter.

   hen duo you piao pia liang de Fang zai gui tai li bian

5. A plate was hung on the wall.

6. Is the door of the post office open? you Ju de men Kai mao dui,
   Yes, it is open.
   Zheng zai Kai zhe o

7. I like to drink coffee while I listen to music.

8. He answered with a smile: "The sender's name and address
   have to be written at the bottom." Ta shou de shou,
   xie...

9. He said while pointing to the chart: "You should write the
   envelope this way." Ta shou zheng zai zhi zhe qiang shong de Tu pian;
   ni zen yong xie xin Feng

10. There are many people in the post office. Some are waiting
    to buy stamps. Some are sitting and writing letters.

hen duo ren you Ju li, you de deng zhe mai you piao, you de zuo zhe

xie xin

Translate into Chinese:

1. While in class, the students listened attentively.

2. He said loudly to me: "Let's go swimming."

3. Do you know why this year's winter is so long?

4. I still do not know how to write some of these words.

5. Some people like to see movies; some like to listen to music.

6. My friend has many stamps. Some are Chinese ones; some are foreign ones.

7. A: Excuse me, how long does it take to send a letter to China?
   B: Regular mail or air mail?
   A: Air mail.
   B: It takes a week.
   A: I want to have it registered too.

Fill in blanks with 着，了，在 or 过.

1. 行李上没有写 _着_ 他的名字.

2. 现在梅花正开 _着_ 呢.
   Flower

3. 我还没用 _过_ 筷子吃中国菜.

4. 五月十五日就要考试 _了_，考试以后就放暑假 _了_.

5. 他以前当 _过_ 老师，现在不当 _了_.

6. 他笑 _着_ 说："我在这儿已经住 _了_ 两年 _了_."

7. 这个字我们学 _过_，可是我又忘 _了_.

8. 我弟弟穿 _着_ 冰鞋正 _在_ 滑冰呢.

9. 你在这儿照相 _了_ 没有?

10. 你在那个食堂吃 _了_ 饭没有?

11. 我昨天去看他的时候，他 _在_ 看电视呢.

Practical Chinese Reader #35 Exercise B

Fill in blanks with 再，又，还 or 就.

1. 放了假，我 __又__ 坐飞机回家了．

2. 今年寒假我工作了一个月，挣了一些钱． 我想利用暑假 ____ 挣
   点钱．

3. 上星期我的表停了，后来好了． 今天我的表 ____ 停了．

4. 我们今天考试了，明天 ____ 要考呢．

5. 我们吃饭以后 ____ 谈吧．

6. 外边 ____ 下雨呢！

7. 那个电影我看过两次． 我想 ____ 看一次．

8. 快十二点了，他 ____ 不想睡．

9. 这一次考试，我考得不好． 我想 ____ 复习一下这一课．

10. 我现在不给家里写信． 我想放假了 ____ 写．

11. 雨已经停了，我们 ____ 要回去了．

28

Answer the following questions:

1. 你的专业是什么？

2. 这学期你给家里写过几次信？

3. 要口语进步应该怎么样？

4. 你说中国话的机会多不多？

5. 你们什么时候放暑假？

6. 今年暑假你想作什么？

7. 你们下学期几月开学？

8. 你了解中国的情况吗？

9. 你们多长时间考一次试？

10. 你学习了汉语以后想作什么？

Translate into Chinese:

1. They took an examination on the fourth day after arriving in Beijing.

2. Some of the students did well in the examination; some did a bit worse.

3. I feel that my speaking skill is not very good. I want to practice listening and speaking more.

4. He made great progress. He can talk with his friends in English now.

5. I was afraid that my parents would be worried. I have written them twice.

6. He used to work in the post office, but he doesn't work there any more.

7. It's December now. We are about to have the winter break.

8. He has been sick for three days. His mother is worried.

9. The doctor carefully checked his heart and said with a smile: "Your heart is normal."

10. I intend to study Chinese for a year here, then I will go to China.

I. Comparative structures with the preposition 比

   A. Comparison is made between two objects with regard to a certain quality which is expressed by a stative verb or a verbal phrase.

   Subj1 + bi + Subj2 + SV/VP
   他　　　比　我　　忙。
   (He is busier than I am.)

   我　　　比　我朋友　了解中国。
   (I have better understanding of China than my friend does.)

   B. Structures with adverbials of degree
       (b's are possible but less frequent.)

   1. a. Subj1 + Verb + de + bi + Subj2 + SV
           他　　　跑　　得　比　我　　　快。
           (He runs faster than I do.)

       b. Subj1 + bi + Subj2 + Verb + de + SV
           他　　　比　我　　跑　　得　　快。
           (He runs faster than I do.)

   2. a. Subj1 + Verb + Obj + Verb + de + bi + Subj2 + SV
           他　　作　菜　作　　得　比　我　　　好。
           (He cooks better than I do.)

       b. Subj1 + Verb + Obj + bi + Subj2 + Verb + de + SV
           他　　作　菜　比　我　　作　　得　好。
           (He cooks better than I do.)

   Note: The negative form 不比 is rarely used out of context.
          It is often used to negate an assertion.

       Eg.   X: 我想他跑得比你快。
                 (I think he runs faster than you do.)

             Y: 不，他跑得不比我快。
                 (No, he doesn't run faster than I do.)

II. Comparative structures with 有/没有

The negative form is used more frequently while the positive form is only used in context.

A.   Subj1 + meiyou + Subj2 + SV/VP
这间房间   没有   那间房间   大。
(This room is not as big as that one.)

我   没有   他   喜欢音乐。
(I don't like music as much as he does.)

B. Structures modified by adverbials of degree
    (b's are possible but less frequent.)

1. a. Subj1 + Verb + de + meiyou + Subj2 + SV
        他   跑   得 没有   我   快。
        (He doesn't run as fast as I do.)

    b. Subj1 + meiyou + Subj2 + Verb + de + SV
        他   没有   我   跑   得 快。
        (He doesn't run as fast as I do.)

2. a. Subj1 + Verb + Obj + meiyou + Subj2 + Verb + de + SV
        我   作   菜 没有   他   作   得 好。
        (I don't cook as well as he does.)

    b. Subj1 + meiyou + Subj2 + Verb + Obj + Verb + de + SV
        我   没有   他   作   菜   作   得 好。
        (I don't cook as well as he does.)

32

I. Give appropriate measure words.

1. 一 ____ 茶具

2. 四 ____ 茶壶

3. 两 ____ 茶碗

4. 这个工厂不生产这 ____ 瓷器.

5. $5.96 = 五 ____ 九 ____ 六 ____

6. 一 ____ 画儿

II. Fill in blanks.

1. 这套茶具比那 ____ 便宜.

2. 这种纸没有那 ____ 薄.

3. 他游泳比我 ____ 得快.

4. 百货大楼的东西比这家商店 ____ 多.

5. 我弟弟画画儿画 ____ 没有我好.

6. 这个茶碗不 ____ 那个高.

7. 你的自行车 ____ 他的高吗? 我的没有他的高.

8. 这种冰鞋一 ____ 多少钱?

9. 这种明信片多少钱一套? 一块三 ____ 六.

10. ____ 比这套便宜的吗? 没有, 这套最便宜.

Rewrite the following sentences by using the worde given in parentheses.

1. 昨天很冷．今天更冷．（比）

2. 这个售货员二十三岁．那个售货员三十岁．（比）

3. 这种瓷器薄．那种瓷器更薄．（不比）

4. 唐山生产瓷器的历史很长．景德镇生产瓷器的历史更长．（没有）

5. 这种自行车的质量好．那种自行车的质量也好．（有）

6. 他每天六点起床．我每天七点起床．（没有）

7. 他复习了五课课文．我复习了三课课文．（比）

8. 我弟弟写字写得好．我妹妹写字也写得好．（有）

9. 他进步得快．我进步得慢．（不比）

10. 我喜欢看电视．我朋友更喜欢看电视．（没有）

Word order:

1. 瓷器　玉　白　纸　薄　那儿的　比　比

2. 质量　提高了　以前　这种茶具的　比

3. 我的　没有　他的　历史知识　多

4. 两个　我　茶壶　要　的　五元

5. 这种表　那种　便宜　有　吗

6. 很长　景德镇　瓷器　的　历史　生产

7. 六个茶碗　一共　四十二　块　毛　四

8. 漂亮　比　这套明信片　有　的　吗

9. 比　他　开车　我　开得　好

10. 我　她　喜欢音乐　没有

Translate into Chinese:

1. This bicycle is cheaper than that one.

2. This kind of jade is not as thin as that kind.

3. Is the quality of this kind of china better than the quality of that kind?

4. Is this tea set as good as that one?

5. Is there anyone in your class who is younger than you are?

6. The painting on this tea pot is prettier than the painting on that one.

7. Things in the Department Store are more expensive than those in this shop.

8. Is England's history longer than China's?

9. My friend studies harder than I do.

10. This college football team does not play as well as that one.

Translate into Chinese:

1. He sings better than I do.

2. My younger sister does not read as many history books as I do.

3. This sales clerk speaks English better than that one.

4. This factory manufactures more tea cups than that one.

5. I do not paint as well as he does.

6. The teachers did not come as early as the students did.

7. A: How much are the postcards per set?
   B: $3.95 per set.
   A: I want two sets. How much are they altogether?
   B: $7.50 for two sets.
   A: Here is a ten dollar bill.
   B: Here is your change, $2.50.

I.   Comparative structures expressing equivalence

A. Subj1 + gen + Subj2 (+ bu) + yiyang (+ SV)
这种布   跟   那种布   一样。
(This kind of material is the same as that kind of material.)

今年的天气 跟   去年   不   一样。
(This year's weather is different from last year's.)

他   跟   我   一样   忙。
(He is as busy as I am.)

B. Subj1 + Verb + Obj + Verb + de + gen + Subj2 + yiyang (+ SV)
他   说   汉语 说   得   跟   中国人 一样。
(He speaks Chinese like a native speaker.)

他   说   汉语 说   得   跟   中国人 一样   好。
(He speaks Chinese as well as a native speaker does.)

II.   Comparative structures with complements of quantity which
      can be non-specific as 一点儿 ('a little'), 得多 ('much
      more'), 一些 ('a little'), or specific.

Subj1 + bi + Subj2 + SV + quantity
今天   比 昨天   冷   一点儿。
(Today is a bit colder than yesterday.)

这种布 比   那种布 好看   一些。
(This kind of material is a little prettier than that kind.)

他弟弟 比 他   年轻   得多。
(His brother is much younger than he is.)

这种笔 比 那种   便宜   五块钱。
(This kind of pen is five dollars cheaper than that kind.)

III. A difference in quantity or time from what was originally
planned or expected may be expressed by the adverbs 多，少，
早，晚 occurring before verbs and quantity.

我多花了十块钱。
(I spent ten dollars more.)

他少买了一张电影票。
(He bought one less movie ticket.)

我只比你早来了五分钟。
(I came only five minutes earlier than you did.)

你先走吧，我要晚走一刻钟。
(You go first. I'll leave fifteen minutes later.)

Fill in blanks with appropriate vocabulary.

1. 这件中山装跟那件 ＿＿＿ ＿＿＿ 肥，可是不 ＿＿＿ ＿＿＿ 长．那件比
   这件长五公分．

2. 我的棉袄的 ＿＿＿ ＿＿＿ 跟你的不一样．我的是蓝的，你的是灰的．

3. 这件衣服的 ＿＿＿ ＿＿＿ 合适吗？ 不 ＿＿＿ ＿＿＿，太短了一些．

4. 这件外衣比那件长 ＿＿＿ ＿＿＿？ 这件比那件长三公分．

5. 这种绸子多少钱一 ＿＿＿？ 三块八一米．

6. 这辆自行车跟那 ＿＿＿ 一样新吗？ 不，那 ＿＿＿ 旧一点儿．

7. 这件雨衣长70公分，那件长72公分． 这件比那件 ＿＿＿ 两公分．

8. 他的表现在是一点五分，我的表是一点十分．我的表比他的 ＿＿＿
   五分钟．

9. 他花了二十块钱，我花了二十五块． 他比我 ＿＿＿ 花了五块钱．

10. 这种茶具十五块一套， 那种三十块一套． 这种茶具比那种
    ＿＿＿ ＿＿＿ 得多．

11. 这双布鞋合适吗？ 小 ＿＿＿ ＿＿＿． 再试试这双．

12. 他吃一个面包，我吃两个面包． 我比他多吃 ＿＿＿ ＿＿＿．

13. 他哥哥二十岁，他十八岁． 他比他哥哥小 ＿＿＿ ＿＿＿ ．

Practical Chinese Reader #37 Exercise B

Word order:

1. 我 一样 高 我朋友 跟

2. 三天 只 多 比 平信 寄 寄 航空信

3. 中山装 蓝色 穿 我 的 有 吗

4. 钱 我 哪儿 应该 交 在

5. 便宜 比 布面的 绸面的 二十块 钱

6. 好 多 我 他 得 游得 游泳 比

7. 瘦 比 我妹妹 我 一点儿

8. 肥 跟 这件 那件 衣服 不一样

9. 两瓶 酒 太多了 请少买

10. 一年中文 比 好 我 只学了 说得 可是 他

Answer the following questions:

1. 你穿多大号的衣服？

2. 你穿几号鞋？

3. 你有多高？

4. 你穿的外衣是中式的，还是西式的？

5. 你喜欢什么颜色？

6. 你爸爸比你妈妈大吗？ 大几岁？

7. 这儿的天气跟你家那儿一样不一样？ 哪儿比较暖和？

8. 你有绸面的中式棉袄吗？

9. 你说汉语说得跟中国人一样吗？

10. 你家的车是什么颜色的？

Translate into Chinese:

1. The color of this cotton tunic suit is the same as that one.

2. The length of this cotton-padded jacket is not the same as the black one.

3. Is the weather here same as the weather in your country?

4. This jacket fits as well as that one.

5. Does he ride a bicycle as fast as you do?

6. Did you spend as much money as he did?

7. This sales clerk speaks English like an Englishman.

8. How much is this kind of fabric per meter?

9. These Western-style suits are $119 per set.

10. The bicycles are $89 each.

Translate into Chinese:

1. This Chinese style cotton-padded jacket is a little bit shorter than that one.

2. The blue sweater is much more loose-fitting than the red one.

3. This kind of silk fabric is five dollars more expensive than that kind.

4. The custom-made table is five centimeters higher than the one you bought.

5. The kind of material I bought is a bit thicker than the kind he bought.

6. This time I paid ten dollars less than last time.

7. My friend spent twenty dollars more than I did.

8. Last month, this factory manufactured one hundred bicycles more than before.

I. Resultative verbs are normally made of two verbs. The first
    element indicates an action and the second element describes
    the result or outcome of the first verb. The second verb
    always has a fixed meaning. Following are some examples.

1. 好: in a good state; properly -- 放好 (to put properly);
        作好 (to do something well); 记好 (to remember well)

2. 错: wrong; by mistake -- 说错 (to say something wrong);
        听错 (did not hear the correct message);
        看错 (did not see correctly)

3. 对: correctly -- 作对 (to do the right thing);
        说对 (to say something correctly);
        拿对 (to get the right thing)

4. 懂: to understand -- 听懂 (to listen and understand);
        看懂 (to understand through reading or seeing);

5. 见: to perceive -- 看见 (to see); 听见 (to hear)

6. 会: to acquire a skill -- 学会 (to master)

Since a resultative verb always describes the result of an action,
i.e., it refers to a completed or expected to be completed event.
imperfective aspect marker 着 therefore never cooccurs with it.
了 is the most likely aspect marker to be employed.

        Subj (+ Neg) + Verb + Comp (+ Asp) + NP (+ le) (+ QD)
        他   看   懂   了   这封信。
        (He read and understood this letter.)

        我   没   看   见   他。
        (I did not see him.)

        他   学   会   开汽车 了   没有?
        (Has he learned how to drive a car yet?)

II. Expressions of direction

        往 + Direction + Verb

        往   前   走。   (Go straight ahead.)

        往   右   拐。   (Turn to the right.)

Fill in blanks with appropriate vocabulary.

1. 请问，到语言学院 怎 么 走？
   please arrived language college how to go or to

2. 从这儿 往 南走，到红绿灯再 往 右拐.
   From there towards Southwalk, arrive traffic light again towards right turn

3. 买两张 到 平安里的票.
   buy two To (Street name) ticket

4. 我要坐开 往 北海公园的车.
   I need to take towards bei hai park bus

5. 换13 路 (公共汽车，在哪儿下车？
   number 13 Bus at there get off bus

6. 这路车的终点) ____ 是平安里.
   This bus Terminal is (pi lan li street)

7. 钢铁学院 离 这儿远不远？ Chpt. 30
   Steele College From thee Far not For

8. 这个字很容易，你 怎 么 没写对？
   This letter very easy you why not write correct

9. 请问这是什么 方 向 ？ 这是东边.
   Please ask this is what direction this is eastern port

10. 上课以前请先 排 队.
    after class before please line up

Any Four

Fill in blanks with appropriate resultative complements:

1. 下飞机的人请带 __hao__ 自己的行李．

2. 今天上午的考试不难，老师的问题我都回答 ____ 了．

3. 我学中文学了快一年了，我能看 ____ 容易的中文书．

4. 今天我不能开车，我的汽车还没修 ____ 呢！

5. 有人敲门，你听 __见__jian__ 了没有？
   Somebody Knocked you

6. 昨天你在学校看 __见__jian__ 了我哥哥没有？
   School

7. 他说汉语说得不清楚，我没有听 __Dong____．

8. 去中国以前，你要先到中国大使馆去办 __hao____ 签证．
   First *Embassy*

9. 收信人的地址不对，你写 __错__cuo__ 了．

10. 我还没学 __会__hui__ 开车，所以我不能开车送你去车站．
    able to

11. 我们写 ____ 练习以后再去看电影吧！

12. 这路车不去百货大搂，你坐 __错__cuo__ 了．
    Gong

13. 这个成语故事你听 ____ 了没有？

Translate into Chinese (using resultative verb complements):

1. The bus is about to start. Please be seated properly.

2. I did not hear correctly the address he gave me.

3. Did you do the exercises correctly?

4. The clerk did not understand (through reading) the characters on the sign.

5. Have you seen the jacket I am looking for?

6. The worker has repaired his bicycle.

7. Sorry I'm late. I took the wrong bus.

8. This question is pretty easy. How come he didn't answer it correctly?

9. How come he didn't understand (by listening) the ticket-seller's questions?

10. I haven't learned how to use chopsticks.

Translate into Chinese:

1. A: Excuse me, how do I get to the department store?
    B: Go south from here. Make a left turn when you get to
        the traffic lights.

2. A: Where is the street-car station?
    B: Go west. Make a right turn at the intersection.

3. A: Two tickets for the Language Institute.
    B: You've taken the wrong bus. The direction is not
        right. You should take the bus which goes east.
    A: What number bus should I take?
    B: You get off at the park and transfer to number 113
        bus.

4. A: How many more stops are there before the terminus?
    B: There are three more stops. Please take your things
        with you when getting off.

5. A: Does this bus go to the Beijing Iron and Steel
        Engineering Institute?
    B: Yes. Please line up to get on the bus.

Gubo （古波） went to see his friend yesterday. Write a short paragraph describing how he got to his friend's house in accordance with the given chart.

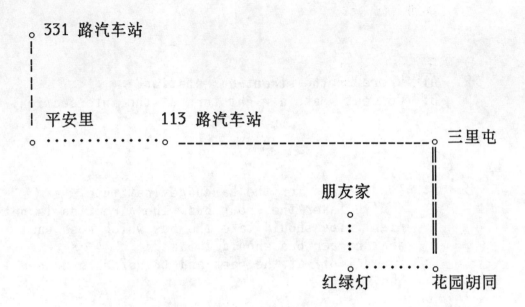

331 路汽车站

平安里　　　　　113 路汽车站

三里屯

朋友家

红绿灯　　　花园胡同

———— 坐公共汽车

…… 走路

======= 坐电车

I. More resultative verbs!

1. 到 -- to succeed in
    找到 (to find); 收到 (to receive); 见到 (to see);
    拿到 (to get)

2. 完 -- to finish
    唱完 (to finish singing); 用完 (to finish using)

3. 住 -- in a fixed or proper state
    记住 (to remember well)

II. Post-verbal prepositions

Post-verbal prepositions are certain verb type words which occur immediately after the main verb in a sentence. These verbs should not be considered as resultative complements, because they are more closely related to the noun phrases following them than to the preceding verbs. They may indicate a location or a recipient. Thus they behave more like pre-verbal prepositions or coverbs such as 从，在，到，把，or 用.

1. 在 -- at, on, in
    放在 (to put in/on/at); 写在 (to write ... on);
    挂在 (to hang on)

2. 到 -- to
    走到 (to walk to); 学到(第三十课) (to study to lesson 30)

3. 往 -- toward
    开往 (to drive toward)

III.   Fronting of definite noun phrases

When a verb with a definite noun phrase as its object is followed by the post-verbal preposition 在, the object is fronted to the beginning of the sentence in which it occurs. For example:

那套明信片我放在桌子上了。
(I placed the set of postcards on the table.)

今天的练习我写在纸上。
(I wrote today's exercises on the paper.)

IV.   Sentence connectives

A.   The construction 一 ... 就 ('as soon as') functions as a connective associating two sentences. Both 一 and 就 must precede a verb. If the subjects of the two sentences are identical, the second one may be deleted.

Subj1 + yi + Predicate1 (+ Subj2) + jiu + Predicate2
我   一   放假   就   回国。
(I will return to my country as soon as the vacation begins.)

他   一   教   大家   就   会了。
(Once he started teaching, everyone learned.)

B.   虽然 ... 但是/可是 -- although ... but

虽然他没来过中国，可是对北京了解得很多。
(Although he has never been to China, he knows a lot about Beijing.)

他虽然没来过中国，但是对北京了解得很多。
(Although he has never been to China, he knows a lot about Beijing.)

I. Fill in blanks with proper verbs and resultative complements.

1. 上午我去宿舍找他，可是没 _____ 他．

2. 上个月我阿姨说要从中国给我来信，我昨天 _____ 她的信了．

3. 我可以用你的词典吗？

    可以，但是 _____ 了请放在我的书桌上．

4. 我妈妈到百货大楼去买那种茶具，可是没 _____，因为他们没有那种茶具．

5. 我在哪儿办手续？　在那儿．_____ 了手续请到对面透视．

6. 老师讲的语法，我记了，可是没 _____，都忘了．

7. 今天下午大学队和工人队赛球．_____ 了以后，大家一起去吃饭．

II. Fill in blanks with proper main verbs and post-verbal prepositions.

1. 我的帽子在哪儿？　你的帽子 _____ 墙上呢！

2. 他的名字，我 _____ 本子上了．

3. 昨天晚上我作练习 _____ 十二点钟．

4. 这学期我们学了很多课汉语．我们现在 _____ 第三十九课了．

5. 你要的那本书我没带来，我 _____ 家里了．

6. 请问，到邮局怎么走？　你 _____ 红绿灯以后，往右拐．

7. 我的外衣，你放好了吗？　我 _____ 箱子里了．

Word order:

1. 邻居 我们 很关心 对 我们的

2. 的 意思 吗 成语 懂 你 这句

3. 了 天气 是 虽然 春天 还是 现在 很冷
已经 但是

4. 弟弟 的 是 叔叔 爸爸

5. 在街上 还能 他 可是 做一些工作 虽然 退休了
已经 他

6. 愉快的 我们 记住 一天 这个 永远 要

7. 笑 小姑娘 了 客人 就 看见 一 这个

8. 吃饭 留 客人 下来 请 远方的

9. 上月 车间主任 当了 他 车间里选举

Answer the following questions according to the content of the text in this lesson.

1. 古波和帕兰卡上星期去丁云家，他们见到了丁云家里的什么人？

2. 丁云她爸爸作什么工作？

3. 丁云的妈妈现在怎么样？

4. 帕兰卡为什么说丁云家的邻居也非常热情？

5. 小兰是谁？ 她今年几岁？

6. 丁云爸爸怎么说他自己？ 那句话是什么意思？

7. 丁云妈妈留古波和帕兰卡吃饭，他们留下来了没有？ 为什么？

8. 那一天古波和帕兰卡过得很愉快. 对那一天，他们要怎么样？

Translate into Chinese:

1. A: Listen! Someone is knocking at the door.
   B: I didn't hear it.

2. A: Did you receive letters from your uncle?
   B: No. But I received a letter from my aunt this morning.

3. A: Have they finished studying this book?
   B: Not yet.

4. This student did not memorize the vocabulary well.

5. I've looked for my notebook all morning, but I didn't find it.

6. Have you received the bicycle he gave you (as present)?

7. It was pretty late when I walked to the station.

8. We have already studied up to lesson thirty.

Translate into Chinese:

1. I put the notebook you bought on the table.

2. Where did you write your neighbor's address?

3. The guests left as soon as we finished eating. Nobody stayed.

4. As soon as he heard this piece of news, he cried.

5. As soon as the retired teacher returned to his home, he saw his younger sister running to the street to welcome him.

6. Although he is smart, he does not understand the meaning of this sentence.

7. Although he said that he would remember that day forever, he soon forgot it all.

Fill in blanks with sentence particles 呢，吧，or 了.

1. 现在是夏天 ____，天气已经很热 ____.

2. A: 今年秋天你要回国 ____?

   B: 不，我不回国，我还要在中国住半年 ____.

3. A: 我们在哪儿下车 ____?

   B: 我们在终点站下车 ____.

4. A: 别看电视 ____，现在已经七点 ____，电影快开始 ____.

   B: 你先走 ____，我不想去看电影 ____.

5. A: 昨天晚上他们在家作什么 ____?

   B: 我去的时候他们正看电视 ____.

6. A: 他们已经拿到表 ____，你们 ____?

   B: 我们也拿到 ____.

7. A: 再吃点 ____.

   B: 谢谢，我已经吃得很多 ____.

8. 我们还没见过面 ____. 你是学生代表王小蓝 ____?

9. 运动会就要开始 ____. 观众都站在操场旁边，可是主席还没到

   主席台上 ____.

10. A: 这次的百米赛他一定能打破记录，你 ____?

    B: 不，我能保持记录就很好 ____.

Fill in blanks with resultative complements.

1. 有人敲门，你听 ____ 了没有？

2. 他激动地说："网球赛已经打 ____ 了，我输了."

3. 观众们鼓 ____ 了掌以后，主席开始说话了.

4. 他跑到百米的终点那儿的时候看 ____ 了很多观众站在那儿.

5. 你听 ____ 广播了吗？没有，太远了，我没听 ____.

6. 那个运动员跑得快极了，他打 ____ 了男子百米赛的记录.

7. 这是谁的表？别拿 ____ 了.

8. 这一课的生词你都记 ____ 了吗？

9. 他找 ____ 了他的照片了没有？

10. 我每天洗 ____ 澡以后才吃早饭.

11. 今天早上他去接他的叔叔，接 ____ 了没有？

Answer the following questions:

1. 你喜欢什么运动?

2. 夏天最好的运动是什么?

3. 你参加过运动会吗?

Jia

4. 你会不会打太极拳?

5. 看运动比赛的时候你激动吗?

6. 你有没有你爸爸高?

7. 今天是不是比昨天冷?

8. 你说汉语说得跟你的老师一样好吗?

You said hanyu spoken with your teacher is similar good

9. 你常常听新闻广播吗?

10. 作完这个练习以后你要作什么?

Translate into Chinese:

1. The audience applauded warmly for the athletes.

2. He does not play Taijiquan.

3. Who got the highest score in this examination?

4. He was very excited during each ball game, but I was even more excited than he was.

5. There are so many people coming to attend the sports meet.

6. This athlete is only 0.1 second faster than the other one.

7. Nobody broke the record in the men's one hundred meter race. Xiao Zhang kept his own record of 11.2 seconds.

8. The athletic field at our school is much bigger than the one at their school.

9. Who is the fastest runner in this sports meet?

10. The tea set she bought is the same as the tea set you bought, but hers was cheaper than yours.

I. Verbs with directional complements: A full-fledged verbal phrase with a directional complement comprises three verbs -- V1 V2 V3.   V1 normally indicates action;   V2 indecates position; V3 expresses direction (toward or away from the speaker). Following are examples of the verbs which may fall into different groups.

> V1: 拿，带，跑，走，寄，送，买，找，请
>
> V2: 进(in)，出(out)，上(up)，下(down)，回(back)，过(over)
>
> V3: 来，去

There are possible combinations of these verbs.

> A. V2V3: 进来，出去，上来，下去，进去，回去，过来，etc.
>
> B. V1V3: 拿来，跑去，走来，寄去，送去，买来，带去，etc.
>
> C. V1V2V3: 拿回来，送过去，带进去，走出来，买过来，etc.

If the verb takes an object, there are two possible structures.

> D. V1 + O + V3: 打电话来，带照相机去，寄一封信去，带行李来
>
> E. V1 + V3 + O: 打来电话，带来一位向导，买来吃的东西，送去一本词典

II. 要是 ... 就 (if ... then): 要是 may either precede or follow a subject while 就 always occurs before a verb.

1. yaoshi + Subj1 + Predicate1 + Subj2 + jiu + Predicate2
   要是　　你　　每天都锻炼，你的身体　就　　会很健康。
   (If you exercise everyday, you will be very healthy.)

2. Subj1 + yaoshi + Predicate1 + Subj2 + jiu + Predicate2
   他　　要是　　不来，　　我们　　就　　去找他。
   (If he does not come, we will go to see him.)

III. Contrast between 才 and 就: A sentence with 才 expresses an event which does not live up to one's expectation, therefore 才 never cooccur with Asp -了. A sentence with 就, on the contrary, indicates events exceeding one's expectation.

> 他八点才来。　　　　(He didn't come until eight o'clock.)
>
> 他八点就来了。　　　(He came as early as eight o'clock.)

I. Fill in blanks with appropriate vocabulary.

1. 昨天我们去长城玩，小张 ___ 我们带来了一位向导.

2. 那个亭子高高地站在山上，___ 人一样.

3. 每天上午到学院的车都很 ___，车上的人多 ___ 了，很多人都没有座位.

4. 我八点从家里 ___ 来，在路上 ___ 了半个小时才到这儿.

5. 我哥哥研究中国历史，他 ___ 中国很了解.

6. 天安门是一个高高的 ___ ___，前边有一个 ___ ___.

7. 我听 ___ 《李自成》是一本有名的 ___ ___，说的是崇祯 ___ ___ 在景山山 ___ 下吊死的故事.

8. 我们在门口等了一 ___ ___，他就进来了.

9. A: ___ ___ ___，我来晚了.

   B: ___ ___ ___，我们也刚到.

II. Fill in blanks with directional complements 来 (Lai) or 去 (qu).

1. 向导 (Xiongdoo / Guide) 和我们都在车上，你快上 来 吧.

2. 照相机在楼下. 你下 去 拿 (na / to take) 吧.

3. 我哥哥从中国寄 ___ 了一本中文小说.

4. 我们在门口等你，你别在房间里说话，快出 ___ 吧.

5. 你看! 我们给你带 ___ 了一些点心.

6. A: 天气真好，我们出 去 (walk) 走走，好吗?

   B: 好啊，可是下午我有事儿，不能回 来 得太晚.

7. 我妹妹在法国，我给她寄 ___ 了五十元.

8. 他们到公园去玩的时候没带照相机 ___.

9. 王主任和我们在里边等你，请进 ___ 吧.

Practical Chinese Reader #41 Exercise B

I. Fill in blanks with 才 or 就.

1. 我们在外边等了很久 __才__ 进来.

2. 我们在外边等了一会儿 __就__ 进来了.

3. 今天车真挤，我们在路上花了一个小时 __才__ 到这儿.

4. 车 __就__ 要开了，请大家上车吧.

5. 我很早 ___ 听说过李自成的故事.

6. 《李自成》这本小说我以前没听说过，到今天 ___ 知道有这本书.

7. 要是我没带照相机，我 ___ 不能照相了.

8. 你们先进教室去，我一会儿 ___ 来.

9. 电影八点 ___ 开始，可是他们六点半 __就__ 到电影院门口了.

10. 你们从东边下山去． 他们 ___ 在山脚下.

11. 要是今天不考试，我 ___ 晚一点再去学院.

12. 秋天了． 树叶 __就__ 要红了.

II. Insert 了 at appropriate positions in the following sentences.

1. 我的同学给我送来两张运动会的票.

2. 你带那本小说来吗?

3. 学生不在这儿． 他们进教室去.

4. 他们去北海玩，带照相机去吗?

5. 我给我姐姐寄一本小说去.

64

Complete the following dialogues:

1. A：对不起，_____．

   B：没关系，_____．

2. A：你怎么现在才来？

   B：_____．

3. A：_____．

   B：我没带来． 我明天给你送去．

4. A：_____．

   B：我们们从西边上山吧．

5. A：我不送了，请慢慢儿走．

   B：谢谢，_____．

6. A：_____．

   B：太好了，你想得真周到．

7. A：_____．

   B：要是明天不下雨，我们就去参观天安门广场．

8. A：今天外边人多极了．

   B：_____．

9. A：星期天你想作什么？

   B：_____ 或者 _____．

Translate into Chinese:

1. The guide is waiting for us at the entrance. Let's go out.

2. The building is in the square. Let's go over there to take a look.

3. Where are the guests? They went downstairs.

4. When will the driver return? We will go up the mountain in a while.

5. Having finished washing the clothes, he came back to the dormitory.

6. Have you brought your camera? Come over and take a picture of the pavilion.

7. I heard that he mailed twenty dollars to his younger brother.

8. I brought some snacks for you guys.

9. The doctor did not come to the infirmary.

10. We will go back home as soon as the semester ends.

Translate into Chinese:

1. If the weather is nice, you can see streets and buildings of Beijing clearly.

2. If I had received my friend's telephone call, I would not have gone out.

3. I didn't know anything about the story of this Chinese emperor until I read this historical novel.

4. The driver did not come back until when we were about to set off.

5. He heard that this novel was in the store. He then went downtown to buy it.

6. A: How come you came so late?
   B: I am sorry. The bus was too crowded. It took me more than an hour to get here.
   A: Have you brought the novel that I wanted?
   B: I left it at home. Either I can send it to you tomorrow or you can pick it up at my home (go to my home to take it) today.
   A: You're very thoughtful, but I'm going back home shortly.

Resultative verbs may be used in two different modes: the actual mode and the potential mode. What we have learned previously are those in actual mode, i.e., they denotes completed or expected to be completed events. The potential mode of the resultative verbs indicates whether a subject is able to cause the result to take place after taking the action.

The potential mode is expressed in the following forms.

A. Positive: V1 + 得 + V2
        听得懂 (be able to listen and understand)
        看得见 (be able to see)
        收得到 (be able to receive)

B. Negative: V1 + bu + V2
        看不完 (be unable to finish reading)
        修不好 (be unable to repair)
        找不到 (be unable to find)

C. Interrogative: V1 得 V2 + V1 不 V2
        作得完作不完 (be able to finish?)
        看得懂看不懂 (be able to read and understand?)

There are certain verbs which belong to V2 category and which occur in a potential mode only.

D. 了 -- to be able to
        完成得了 (be able to finish)
        用不了 (be unable to use up)
        回答不了 (be unable to answer)
        实现得了 (be able to carry out)

E. 下 -- to accommodate
        放得下 (be able to store)
        挂得下 (have the space to hang)
        坐得下 (be able to seat)

F. 动 -- to move
        跑得动 (have the energy to run)
        骑不动 (be unable to ride)
        跳不动 (be unable to jump)

Verbs with directional complements may also take potential mode.

G. 上得去 (be able to go up)
    进不来 (be unable to come in)

Fill in blanks with resultative verb complements.

1. 你说得太快，我听不 _____.

2. 汽车挤得 _____ 八个人吗?

3. 那个书店里买得 _____ 《李自成》吗?

4. 这些活儿，那个退休的老工人干得 _____ 干不 _____?

5. 这个城太小了，看不 _____ 中国电影.

6. 你吃得 _____ 这么多东西吗?

7. 天气预报说，明天会下雨，我们去得 _____ 去不 _____ 公园?

8. 这张椅子太重，你搬*不 _____ 吧.

9. 我的裙子在哪儿? 我不知道. 我找不 _____.

10. 这个广场停得 _____ 多少车?

11. 东西这么多，你拿得 _____ 拿不 _____?

12. 自行车太旧了，我想我修不 _____.

13. 箱子这么小，放得 _____ 这么多的东西吗?

14. 他身体不好，明天参加不 _____ 运动会了.

15. 衣服太多了，我洗不 _____.

16. 天安门广场站得 _____ 一百万人.

17. 这些工作你完成得 _____ 完成不 _____?

18. 我还看不 _____ 中文杂志.

19. 练习很多，你作得 _____ 吗?

20. 你写的字太小了，我看不 _____.

69

I. Fill in blanks with appropriate potential resultative verbs.

1. 山上的亭子你 _____ 吗？　　太远了，我 _____.

2. 这本小说你 _____ 吗？　　我的英文不好，我 _____.

3. 这些生词你 _____？　　生词不多，我 _____.

4. 今天老师给的练习你 _____ _____？

　　　　练习太难了，我 _____.

5. 在美国你们 _____ 中国菜吗？

　　　　美国有很多中国饭馆，我们 _____ 中国菜.

6. 今天照的照片你 _____ _____？

　　　　照片不太多，我想我 _____.

7. 那个正在修建的礼堂，明年 _____ 吗？

　　　　工人很多，我想 _____.

8. 箱子这么重，你 _____ 吗？

　　　　这个箱子不太重，我 _____.

9. 这辆自行车你 _____ 吗？

　　　　没问题，我一定 _____.

10. 桌子这么大，你 _____ 吗？

　　　　我一个人 _____.

11. 这间房间 _____ 四个人吗？

　　　　房间太小，_____ 四个人.

12. 这些活儿，你一个人 _____ _____？

　　　　活儿太重了，我一个人 _____.

II. Fill in blanks with proper words of measurement.

1. 这个尺有多 ____? 一米.

2. 这个房间有多 ____? 二十平方米*.

3. 这张桌子有多 ____? 三十公斤*.

4. 这位老爷爷今年多 ____ 岁数了? 他今年六十九岁.

5. 这个门有多 ____ ? 三米.

6. 这块布有多 ____ ? 一尺.

III. Write out the figures in Chinese characters.

1. 6,428 _____

2. 9,730 _____

3. 5,200 _____

4. 20,000 _____

5. 45,000 _____

6. 91,326 _____

Answer the following questions:

1. 天安门有多高?

2. 天安门广场站得下多少人?

3. 广场中间是什么? 西边是什么? 东边有什么?

4. 人民大会堂里边的大礼堂有多大? 一共几层?

5. 人民大会堂是哪年修建的? 用了多长时间完成的?

6. 人民大会堂坐得下多少人?

7. 人民大会堂是现代建筑还是古代建筑?

8. 典型的中国古代建筑有些什么?

9. 你们学院有多少学生?

10. 美国有多少人口(population)?

Translate into Chinese:

1. The film can't be developed by evening.

2. Can you see the pavilion on the hill?

3. I was unable to find the construction site you mentioned.

4. This car can seat five people.

5. The worker was unable to do such a heavy job.

6. There are so many things. Are you able to take them?

7. A: How tall is your younger brother?
    B: He is one hundred and senventy-nine centimeters tall.

8. A: How big is this auditorium?
    B: This auditorium is forty meters wide, and fifty meters long. It can accommodate several thousand people.

9. Although he is eighty years old, he can still walk around, hear things, and see things clearly.

10. A: How come you did not go into the auditorium?
    B: There were many people in the doorway. I could not get in.

I. More about verbs and their directional complements!

Verbal phrases which have the form V1V2V3 (see #41 Grammar Notes) may take a noun phrase as object or a place word as destination.

A. Place words as destinations

Subj (+ OE) + V1 + V2 + Place + V3 + OE
他　　　　　跑　上　楼　　去　了。
(He went upstairs.)

汽车　不能　　开　进　公园里　来。
(Cars are not allowed to drive into the park.)

B. When the verb of a sentence takes a direct object, there are two possibilities.

1. Subj (+ OE) + V1 + V2 + V3 + Object (+ OE)
他　给你　带　回　来　那本小说　了。
(He has brought back that novel for you.)

2. Subj (+ OE) + V1 + V2 + Object + V3
他　每星期　寄　回　一封信　去。
(He sends a letter back every week.)

II. The coordinator 又 ... 又
                (both ... and; not only ... but also)

又 ... 又 is used to connect two verbal phrases. It must connect two expressions of the same nature, i.e., they must belong to the same grammatical category.

Subj + you + SV1/VP1 + you + SV2/VP2
他心里　又　高兴　　又　难过。
(He feels both happy and sad.)

今天　　又　刮风　　又　下雨。
(Not only is it windy, but it is also raining.)

Practical Chinese Reader #43 Exercise A

Fill in blanks with appropriate vocabulary.

1. A: 我 ＿＿＿＿ 累 ＿＿＿＿ 饿，我们找一 ＿＿＿＿ 饭馆吃饭吧.

   B: 我也有 ＿＿＿＿ ＿＿＿＿ 饿了.

2. 你看，穿 ＿＿＿＿ 马路，那儿有一 ＿＿＿＿ 小吃店，我们过去看看吧!

3. 这是一家北京 ＿＿＿＿ ＿＿＿＿ 的小吃店，里边坐着很多 ＿＿＿＿ ＿＿＿＿.

4. 小吃店里有 ＿＿＿＿ 种小吃，都是北京风味的.

5. A: 你们二位吃 ＿＿＿＿ 什么?

   B: ＿＿＿＿ 四个油饼，两 ＿＿＿＿ 炸糕.

6. 要是不 ＿＿＿＿，再来一碗豌豆粥，＿＿＿＿ ＿＿＿＿ ＿＿＿＿?

7. 别 ＿＿＿＿ 中国菜我也吃过，可是我比 ＿＿＿＿ 喜欢吃北京风味的中

   国菜.

8. 英国人喝茶跟中国人不一样，他们喜欢加 ＿＿＿＿ ＿＿＿＿ 和 ＿＿＿＿.

9. 这家饭馆的服务员都很 ＿＿＿＿ ＿＿＿＿，服务也很 ＿＿＿＿ ＿＿＿＿. 我们

   走的时候，他们还请我们 ＿＿＿＿ 意见.

10. 这是杏仁豆腐，你 ＿＿＿＿ ＿＿＿＿，作得好不好?

11. 你 ＿＿＿＿ ＿＿＿＿ 饿了吗? 怎么不多吃一点?

Fill in blanks with complex directional complements:

1. 礼堂门口怎么站着这么多的人？ 我们走 _____ 看看吧！

2. 一个孩子从屋里跑 _____，大声叫道："爸爸，你回来了."

3. "那幅画，挂在墙上了吗？"

   "已经挂 _____ 了."

4. 别站着说话，大家坐 _____ 谈吧！

5. 那张桌子，你从外边搬 _____ 了吗？

6. 他从箱子里拿 ____ 两件衬衫 ____.

7. 主席从门口走 ____ 礼堂 ____ 的时候，我们都站了 _____.

8. 我请弟弟从邮局买 _____ 二十张邮票.

9. 那个牌子已经从门上拿 _____ 了.

10. （在饭馆里）"菜太多了，吃不完."

    "没关系，吃不完我们可以带 _____."

11. 前边是绿灯*，我们可以快一点开 _____.

12. 我们都不在屋里，你快走 _____ 吧！

13. 我昨天没从老师那儿拿 ____ 本子 ____.

14. 写好的信你寄 _____了没有？

15. 我们今天可以去看京剧了. 小张昨天给我们送 _____ 两张票.

Translate into Chinese:

1. Who has walked in (here) from outside?

2. He did not run out (there).

3. The customer has walked into the restaurant.

4. The athlete swam across the river (to us).

5. Did you buy and bring some snacks back from the snack shop?

6. What did you bring back from school?

7. He did not take the camera back (here).

8. As for the letter, I've sent it out already.

9. The chef (master worker) brought out two fried cakes.

10. A: I feel both hungry and tired.
    B: Don't stand there. Sit down.

Translate into Chinese:

1. He took out two shirts from the suitcase.

2. Cars are not allowed to drive into the park.

3. A: I'm a bit hungry. Let's go into the snack shop to have
      something.
   B: O.K.
   C: What would you like to eat?
   B: Is there a menu*?
   C: Yes. Here it is.
   A: This restaurant has all kinds of Beijing style snacks.
   B: Give us two deep-fried pancakes and two bowls of almond
      junket.
   C: Anything else?
   A: No. Your service is superb.
   C: It's our duty.

Write a short script describing a scene in a Chinese restaurant.

Suggested vocabulary: 服务员，顾客，菜单*，饿，渴*，汽水，好吃，别的，风味．

I. 是 ... 的 as a focus marker

是 may be placed before an element with 的 usually occurring
at the end of a sentence to express that the element is the
focus of the sentence where it occurs. The element can be a
subject, a place word, a time expression, a prepositional
phrase indicating manner, or a verb phrase. The construction
is used with the presupposition that an event has taken place
and the speaker intends to know or to give more information
about it.

A.   Subj + 是 + Time + Predicate + 的

   X. 我母亲　　　　　　　　　　到中国去了。
      (My mother went to China.)

   Y. 她　　是　什么时候　去　　　　的?
      (WHEN did she go?)

   X. 她　　是　上星期　去　　　　的。
      (She went last week.)

B.   他是从上海来的。
      (It was from Shanghai that he came.)

      我们是坐飞机去的。
      (It was by air that we went.)

      他们不是来工作的。
      (They did not come to work.)

      是张老师给我们介绍颐和园的。
      (It was Prof. Zhang who told us about the Summer
       Palace.)

Note: When a verb takes an object, 的 may occur either inbetween
     the verb and its object or at the end of a sentence. For
     example:

     他是什么时候去的广州?

     他是什么时候去广州的?

II.   Sentences with subject-verb reversion are those where
      expressions of location are more emphasized.

      Location + VP + NP
      他家　　　　来了　　几位客人。
      (There were several guests at his house.)

      从车里　　　走下来　　几个人。
      (There came several people from the car.)

III. Exclamatory sentences are expressed by 多(么) ... 啊, or by
      太 ... 了。

      Subj　　　+　duo(mo)/tai　+　SV　+　Particle
      那位服务员　　　　多　　　　　热情　　啊！
      (How nice that clerk is!)

      这儿的风景　　　　多么　　　　美　　　啊！
      (How beautiful the scenery is!)

              太　　　　　好　　　了！
              (That is terrific!)

IV.   只有 ... 才 (only when ... then) connects two sentences.
      Both 只有 and 才 are placed before a verb if the subjects
      of the sentences in question are identical.   只有 occurs at
      the beginning of the first sentence if the two subjects have
      different referents.

  A. Subj + zhiyou + Predicate1 (+ Subj) + cai + Predicate2
     你　　　只有　　　自己去看看，(你)　　才　能了解那儿的情况。
     (Only when you take a look yourself can you understand the
     condition there.)

  B. zhiyou + Subj1 + Predicate1 + Subj2 + cai + Predicate2
     只有　　他　　来，　　　我们　才　　　能去。
     (Only when he comes can we go.)

V.   SV + 得 + VP   (so SV that ... VP)

他难过得哭了起来。
(He was so sad that he started to cry.)

她累得不能走路。
(She was so tired that she could not walk at all.)

Fill in blanks with appropriate vocabulary.

1. 秋天来了，叶子都红了． 外边的 ＿＿＿ ＿＿＿ 很美，像一 ＿＿＿
   画儿一样．

2. 春天的时候，地上的绿 ＿＿＿ 都长出来了．

3. ＿＿＿ 山是一种很好的运动．

4. ＿＿＿ ＿＿＿ 每天从东边出来，从西边下去．

5. 这几年中国和美国的 ＿＿＿ ＿＿＿ 很多．

6. 昆明湖后边是一 ＿＿＿ 山，叫万寿山．

7. 我们的中文一天 ＿＿＿ 一天进步．

8. A：明天你们去颐和园玩，我作你们的向导．

   B：太好 ＿＿＿！

9. 你看！这儿的风景多么美 ＿＿＿！

10. 明年夏天我决定到中国去 ＿＿＿ 行．

11. A：你常常出去看电影吗？

    B：不，只有星期六晚上我 ＿＿＿ 出去看电影．

12. 他们不 ＿＿＿ 来度假*的，他们 ＿＿＿ 来谈贸易的．

13. 他听了以后高兴得跳 ＿＿＿ ＿＿＿．

14. 颐和园是有名的古典 ＿＿＿ ＿＿＿．

15. 冬天来了．天气一天比 ＿＿＿ ＿＿＿ 冷了．

Following sentences are possible answers to certain questions.
Give an appropriate quertion form to each of them.

1. 我是上星期去的颐和园.

2. 我弟弟是一九七五年生的.

3. 他们是坐飞机从广州到北京的.

4. 他是跟两个同学一起到昆明旅行的.

5. 他们这次是来参观工厂的.

6. 我不是从公园去的. 我是从饭馆去的.

7. 草地上坐着几个年轻人.

8. 你只有自己去看看，才能了解到那儿的情况.

9. 我不是骑车来的.

10. 湖边有一个亭子.

Answer questions on the basis of the text:

1. 颐和园是哪一年开始修建的？

2. 万寿山为什么叫这个名字？

3. 万寿山上有什么？

4. 颐和园里的长廊有多长？

5. 长廊上边有什么？

6. 哪儿有一个白塔？

7. 古波说的山上的画儿是什么？

8. 你看过《三国演义》吗？ 那是一本什么样的小说？

9. 昆明湖在哪儿？

Translate into Chinese:

1. It was last week that her mother came.

2. It was with a tourist group that they traveled.

3. When was it that he decided to come with the trade delegation?

4. It was by boat that they went to Japan.

5. The car came from behind.

6. From the lakeside, an old man walked toward us here.

7. From the car, several people walked out.

8. How cordial the sales clerk is!

9. How beautiful the scenery here is!

Translate into Chinese:

1. Nobody knows how much he likes Chinese paintings.

2. Only when the sun is out is Kunming Lake as bright as a mirror.

3. Only when you speak more, listen more, and read more can you learn a foreign language well.

4. Only when you walk to the lakeside can you see the bridge.

5. He was so sad that he began to cry.

6. She was so happy that she shouted loudly: "That's great!"

7. I feel that Chinese is becoming more interesting everyday.

8. The quality of this type of chinaware has been improved year by year.

Fill in blanks with 的，地 or 得.

1. 熊猫吃 ＿＿＿＿ 是竹叶．他们在竹林里不停 ＿＿＿＿ 走来走去．

2. 观众看见了可爱 ＿＿＿＿ 熊猫都热烈 ＿＿＿＿ 鼓掌．

3. 从山上 ＿＿＿＿ 公园看过去，山下 ＿＿＿＿ 建筑看 ＿＿＿＿ 清清楚楚．

4. 见到了从国外回来 ＿＿＿＿ 朋友，他高兴 ＿＿＿＿ 跳了起来．

5. 这儿 ＿＿＿＿ 风景真美！青 ＿＿＿＿ 山，绿 ＿＿＿＿ 水，远远 ＿＿＿＿ 山

   上还有一个亭子．

6. 每个学生都认真 ＿＿＿＿ 在图书馆里学习．

7. 孩子们高高兴兴 ＿＿＿＿ 到学校去了．

8. 她女儿有一双大大 ＿＿＿＿ 眼睛，非常像她妈妈．

9. 今天照 ＿＿＿＿ 照片洗 ＿＿＿＿ 好吗？

10. 他们不是来工作 ＿＿＿＿，他们是来旅行 ＿＿＿＿．

11. 熊猫 ＿＿＿＿ 样子又可爱又可笑．肥肥 ＿＿＿＿ 身体，短短 ＿＿＿＿

   腿，眼睛上像戴着墨镜．

12. 雪下 ＿＿＿＿ 这么大，我们出 ＿＿＿＿ 去吗？

Fill in blanks with 才 or 就.

1. 车 ＿＿＿ 要开了，请大家坐好．

2. ＿＿＿ 他一个人来，别人都出去玩儿了．

3. 只有作完功课以后，我们 ＿＿＿ 能出去看电影．

4. 我 ＿＿＿ 有一件绿衬衫．

5. 我找了半个多小时 ＿＿＿ 找到你家．

6. 他昨天跳舞跳得太晚了． 今天上午十点钟 ＿＿＿ 起床．

7. 他三岁的时候 ＿＿＿ 跟母亲到外国去了．

8. 要是明天是晴天，我们 ＿＿＿ 到颐和园去玩儿．

9. 昨天上午我们没回宿舍，到晚上吃完了饭以后我们 ＿＿＿ 回去．

10. 昨天吃了晚饭以后，我们 ＿＿＿ 去听音乐了．

11. 你从这儿往西走，过两个路口，＿＿＿ 可以看见那个小吃店了．

12. 我们又累又饿，在小吃店里吃了四个油饼，六块炸糕，两碗豆

腐汤 ＿＿＿ 回家．

Give negative forms for the following sentences:

1. 他说汉语说得很流利.

2. 这个工厂的工人工作得跟那个工厂的工人一样认真.

3. 我昨天从箱子里找出一条裙子来.

4. 在那个书店里买得到这本英文小说.

5. 我在动物园看过两次熊猫.

6. 熊猫的样子比别的动物可爱.

7. 他们是跟贸易团到广州来的.

8. 从非洲来的学生跟从南亚来的一样多.

9. 那个礼堂坐得下五千人.

10. 我们作完了练习才去看电影.

11. 那张桌子两个人搬得动.

Translate into Chinese:

1. A: Did you hear what the chairman said?
   B: No, the platform is too far away. I was unable to hear clearly.

2. There were so many people in the zoo. We could not get in.

3. A: How big is the table?
   B: It's five feet long, three feet wide.

4. The look of a panda is both lovely and funny.

5. As soon as she saw her daughter, she was so excited that she began to cry.

6. I've brought a tour guide for you.

7. If your sister does not come and take the camera, we will then mail it to her.

8. That novel was written ten years ago. He has not written any book since then.

把-Construction

A sentence with Ba-construction emphasizes how an object of a sentence is disposed or handled. In a 把-sentence the object of a verb is preposed to the position before the verb and after 把 to form a prepositional phrase. For example:

Subject (+Adv/Neg) + Ba + Object + Verb + Aspect/Complement

他   把 衣服   洗   干净了。
(He washed the clothes.)
你   把 录音机 带   来了   吗?
(Did you bring the tape-recorder?)
(请)你   把 窗户   开   开。
(Please open the window.)
我   把 这件事儿 忘   了。
(I forgot this matter.)
你   把 名字   写   一写。
(Write your name.)
他   没   把 信   写   得很好。
(He did not write the letter well.)
我   明天   把 照相机 带   来。
(I will bring the camera tomorrow.)
向导   把 那个学生 带   来了。
(The guide has brougnt the student here.)

There are several noticeable features about a Ba-sentence:

1.   The verb must be an action verb. Verbs such as 喜欢，有，是，知道，etc. can not occur in a Ba-structure.

2.   The object must be a definite noun, i.e., it must have a referent.

3.   The verb connot stand alone, i.e., the verb must be followed by other element(s). The element(s) may simply be an aspect marker 了 or 着, or a directional complemnent, a quantitative verb modifier, a degree adverbial, or a resultative complement.

4.   Negation 不/没有 is placed before the preposition 把. Other expressions such as time expressions or modals also occur before the preposition.

Fill in blanks with appropriate vocabulary.

I. 帕兰卡昨天晚上睡觉的时候没把窗户 ＿＿＿＿ 上，今天可能感 ＿＿＿＿ 了。她觉得很不 ＿＿＿＿ ＿＿＿＿ ，头 ＿＿＿＿ ，咳 ＿＿＿＿ ，又发 ＿＿＿＿ ，病得很厉 ＿＿＿＿ 。

她到 ＿＿＿＿ ＿＿＿＿ 去看大夫。大夫给她 ＿＿＿＿ 了体温，说是重感冒，要 ＿＿＿＿ 院。听了大夫的话，她 ＿＿＿＿ ＿＿＿＿ 办住院手续，在病房里躺了一天，＿＿＿＿ 了药，＿＿＿＿ 了针以后，已经 ＿＿＿＿ 多了。

II. 1. 请把门开 ＿＿＿＿ 。

2. 我已经把电视关 ＿＿＿＿ 了。

3. 你把我带来的录音听一 ＿＿＿＿ 吧。

4. 你把饺子包 ＿＿＿＿ 了吗？

5. 请他把带去的东西检查 ＿＿＿＿ ＿＿＿＿ 。

6. 请护士* 把病人的体温量一 ＿＿＿＿ 。

7. 你把花儿都种 ＿＿＿＿ 了没有？

8. 妈妈把衣服都洗 ＿＿＿＿ 了。

9. 你把药吃 ＿＿＿＿ 没有？

10. 他没把我的照相机带 ＿＿＿＿ 。

Change the following sentences into sentences with 把-construction.

1. 请你立刻开开录音机，我想听听。

2. 昨天晚上我没关上窗户，所以感冒了。

3. 这件事儿，他们告诉了我。

4. 大夫请护士* 量一量他的体温。

5. 姥姥包好了饺子，大家就开始吃了。

6. 录音机录上了他说的话。

7. 他忘了吃药了，所以病没好。

8. 那张照片你还给了他没有？

9. 请拿出挂号证* 来。

10. 葡萄他没洗干净。

Answer questions with 把-construction.

1. 我的录音机怎么不见了？

2. 他送来的葡萄在哪儿？

3. 病房里为什么这么冷？

4. 电视机还开着吗？

5. 你给你朋友寄去了什么？

6. 大夫对你作了些什么？

7. 我的衣服在哪儿？

8. 我要带走的东西怎么了？

9. 我们什么时候可以吃饺子？

Practical Chinese Reader #46 Exercise D

I. Translate into Chinese:

Doctor: What's wrong with you?

Patient: I have a headache, and a cough too. It's very likely
         that I have a cold.

Doctor: Let me take your temperature. Open your mouth.

Patient: Do I have a fever?

Doctor: Yes, but not too serious. How long have you had the
         discomfort?

Patient: Last evening.

Doctor: You have a cold. You will feel better after taking
         some medicine. here's the prescription.

Patient: How should I take the medicine?

Doctor: Four times a day, two tablets each time.

Patient: Thank you.

II. Controlled composition.

Write a paragraph in Chinese about your experience of seeing a
doctor. You thought you caught a cold and explained to your
doctor what happened. The doctor did the routine check-up on
you. You did not get better after having taken the medicine
prescribed by the doctor. However, you finally got better
because of some other measures.

(You finish the story.)

I. 把-construction

把-construction must be employed in cases where resultative verbs or verbs with post-verbal prepositions take definite nouns as their objects.

A. Verbs with post-verbal prepositional phrases

在 -- at, in, on
他把笔忘在家里了。   (He left his pen at home.)
你把书放在哪儿了?   (Where did you put the book?)

到 -- to
我把椅子拿到楼上去了。   (I took the chair upstairs.)
他们把我送到车站。   (They saw me to the station.)

给 -- to
我把钱交给了售票员。
(I gave the money to the ticket seller.)
请把书留给他。
(Please leave the book to him.)

B. Verbs with resultative complements

成 -- into; for
他想把房子修建成那个样子。
(He intends to build the house like that.)
我把他看成了中国人。
(I took him for a Chinese.)

作 -- as
他们把他看作家里人。
(They consider him as a family member.)
上海人把 "喝茶" 叫作 "吃茶"。
(People in Shanghai refer to "喝茶" as "吃茶".)

II.   除了 ... (以外) ... 还 (in addition to)
       除了 ... (以外) ... 都 (except)

A. 昨天下午除了游泳，他还钩鱼了。
    (Yesterday afternoon he fished in addition to swimming.)

B. 除了他骑自行车去以外，我们都坐车去了。
    (We all went by car but he rode a bicycle.)

96

Fill in blanks with suitable vocabulary:

1. 鲁迅的故居的院子里有两 ____ 枣树.

2. 这 ____ 房子有三 ____ 卧室.

3. 我看过一 ____ 鲁迅写的文章，也看过他写的一 ____ 小说.

4. 美国诗人 Emily Dickinson 的 ____ ____ 在麻州安城.

5. 去年我到中国去了． 回来以后，我很 ____ ____ 在中国的生活.

6. 参观了有名的人的故居以后，很多人把 ____ ____ 写在留言簿上.

7. 除了他们俩 ____ ____，别的人 ____ 喜欢爬山.

8. 房子的北边 ____ 着另一个房子.

9. 这句话我看不懂，请你给我 ____ ____ 一下.

10. ____ ____ 历史以外，我 ____ 喜欢艺术.

11. 鲁迅给中国人民留下了 ____ ____ 的文化遗产.

Fill in blanks with 成，作，在，到，or 给．

1. 北京人把 ice-lolly 叫 ____ 冰棍儿．

2. 老师把这个伟大的文学家的生活介绍 ____ 我们．

3. 我们把两株树种 ____ 院子里．

4. 对不起，我忘了把书带 ____ 学校里来，我把书留 ____ 家里了．

5. 我把他给我的照片留 ____ 纪念*．

6. 父母都想把孩子培养 ____ 好青年．

7. 请把句子翻译 ____ 中文．

8. 大家把他选 ____ 主席．

9. 他们把车开 ____ 飞机场去接他．

10. 我已经把练习交 ____ 老师了．

11. 这个设计师 (designer) 把礼堂设计 ____ 现在这个样子．

12. 请你把这件行李带 ____ 我哥哥请他寄 ____ 中国去．

13. 那个老人把这个年轻人看 ____ 自己的儿子．

14. 他父亲的遗产都留 ____ 了他．

15. 他把 '大夫' 念 ____ 了 'dafu'．

Make sentences:

1. 把 ... 看作

2. 把 ... 作成

3. 把 ... 留给

4. 把 ... 拿到

5. 把 ... 叫作

6. 除了 ... 以外 ... 也

7. 除了 ... 以外 ... 都

8. 除了 ... 以外 ... 还

Translate into Chinese:

1. They wrote their names in the visitor's book.

2. I have already returned the book to the library.

3. They spent ten years developing the small clinic into a hospital.

4. They did not say "good-bye" to me until they saw me off at the station.

5. My classmates asked me to bring the tape-recorder to you.

6. They elected this worker to be director of the factory.

7. Everyone got the flu except him.

8. Besides this article, what other writings of Lu Xun's have you read?

9. The weather here is pretty good except (the fact that) it is a bit cold in winter.

10. The guide led the visitors to the courtyard.

Interrogative pronouns (IP) which have general denotations

A.   As subjects

IP   +   都/也   (+ Neg) + Predicate
谁   都   不   想睡觉。
(Nobody would like to sleep.)

什么   都   好。
(Anything is good.)

哪儿   都   有人。
(There are people everywhere.)

B.   As objects

Subject + IP   +   都/也   (+ Neg)   +   Predicate
他   什么   都   想试一试。
(He would like to try anything.)

这位作家   哪个国家   都   去过。
(This writer has been to every country.)

Fill in blanks with vocabulary:

1. 中国的春节就 ＿＿＿＿ 圣诞节一样，是 ＿＿＿＿ 家人团聚的 ＿＿＿＿ ＿＿＿＿.

2. 春节的时候见到别人要给人 ＿＿＿＿ 年.

3. 在春节的时候，常常可以看到 "恭 ＿＿＿＿ 新 ＿＿＿＿" 这四个字.

4. 新年的时候，全家人在一起 ＿＿＿＿ 年. 孩子们都 ＿＿＿＿ 新衣服，新
   鞋，＿＿＿＿ 新帽子，在外边 ＿＿＿＿ 爆竹，＿＿＿＿ 灯笼，高兴 ＿＿＿＿ 了.

5. 中国新年是 ＿＿＿＿*历正月 ＿＿＿＿ ＿＿＿＿.

6. 春节的前一晚叫作 ＿＿＿＿ ＿＿＿＿*.

7. 吃年夜饭*是中国人的 ＿＿＿＿ ＿＿＿＿.

8. 春节的时候，很多人在门上 ＿＿＿＿ 春联，在墙上 ＿＿＿＿ 年画儿.

9. 吃年夜饭的时候，桌上总是 ＿＿＿＿ 着很多菜.

10. 我真 ＿＿＿＿ 想 ＿＿＿＿ 他写字写得这么整齐.

11. A：您要的东西我都带来了.

    B：谢谢您，真太 ＿＿＿＿ ＿＿＿＿ 您了.

12. 他家里总是 ＿＿＿＿ 扫得很 ＿＿＿＿ 净.

13. A：他 ＿＿＿＿ ＿＿＿＿ ＿＿＿＿ 没有回家？

    B：＿＿＿＿ ＿＿＿＿ 最近比较忙，所以没有回家.

Complete the following sentences by supplying verbal phrases and make them sentences with a passive meaning.

1. 过年的饭菜

2. 这篇文章

3. 我买来的花儿

4. 客人的房间

5. 他带来的新年礼物

6. 桌上的东西

7. 你朋友要的春联

8. 孩子们的爆竹

9. 邮票都

Complete the following sentences with the given interrogative pronouns.

1. 全班除了这个学生以外，_____ （谁）

2. 除了鱼以外，_____ （什么菜）

3. 明天我全天都有空儿 _____ （什么时候）

4. 我的车坏了，还没修好，所以 _____ （哪儿）

5. 菜已经作好了，但是 _____ （谁）

6. 练习太多了，_____ （怎么）

7. 昨天我去百货大楼买东西，可是人太多了，所以 _____

_____ （什么）

8. 你知道谁想要这件礼物？_____ （谁）

9. 谁想去中国参观？_____ （哪个作家）

10. 春节的时候哪儿可以看到年画儿？_____ （哪儿）

Answer the following questions:

1. 春联最常贴在哪儿？

2. 春联都是用什么纸写的？

3. 在美国，新年的时候放爆竹吗？

4. 春节为什么要放爆竹？

5. 为什么中国人吃年夜饭的时候要吃鱼？

6. 今年圣诞节你和谁一起过的？

7. 今年新年你过得怎么样？

8. 你看过中国年画儿吗？

Translate into Chinese:

1. The room has not been cleaned up yet.

2. The lantern with the characters "Happy New Year" written on it has been hung up.

3. All the food for the New Year have been prepared.

4. Pandas are lovely animals. Everyone likes them.

5. I did not realize that he ate nothing but American food.

6. He will read books by any writer, since he loves reading.

7. I heard that people here eat dumplings at New Year, but you may have them any day.

8. We came late today because we went to bed a bit late last night.

9. I did not buy that lamp, because I did not bring enough money with me.

10. Since this winter is relatively mild, I spent my Christmas at home.

I. Sentences of passive voice

Recipient + Neg + Prep + Actor + Verb + OE
我的自行车　　　　让　他　　骑　　走了。
(My bicycle was ridden away by him.)

我们　都　　被　　这个作品　感动　　了。
(We were all moved by this literary work.)

我的纸　　没　叫　风　　刮　　走。
(My paper was not blown away by the wind.)

照相机　　　　被　　他们　　拿　　走了吗?
(Was the camera taken away by them?)

II. The connective 不但 ... 而且 connects either two predicates
or two sentences. Its position of occurrence varies.

A. Subject + 不但 + Predicate1 + 而且 + Predicate2
这个话剧　不但　写得好，　　　而且　　演得也很好。
(This play was not only well written but well performed.)

B. 不但 + Subj1 + Predicate1 + 而且 + Subj2 + Predicate2
不但　中国人　怀念他　　而且　外国人　也怀念他。
(Not only did the Chinese miss him, but foreigners missed
him too.)

III. 连 ... 也/都 (even) may apply to

A. a subject

连 + Subject + 都/也 + Predicate
连　孩子们　都　　被吸引住了。
(Even the children were enchanted.)

连　这位作家　也　　来了。
(Even this writer has come.)

B. an object

Subj + 连 + Obj + 都/也 + Predicate
他　连　衣服　也　没有换。
(He did not even change his clothes.)

她　连　椅子　都　带来了。
(She even brought the chair with her.)

Fill in blanks with appropriate vocabulary.

1. ____ ____ 是记一个人一天的事或者感想.

2. 这个话剧要在那个很大的 ____ ____ 演出.

3. 那个话剧的 ____ ____ 非常成功.

4. 作家，画家，演员*都是 ____ ____ 家.

5. 《茶馆》是老舍写的有名的 ____ ____ 之一.

6. 他的小说我以前看过，但是看他的话剧这 ____ 是第一次.

7. 请你给我正 ____ 的回答.

8. 中国的旧社会是一个黑 ____ 的社会.

9. 我们不但被这个话剧吸 ____ 住了，____ ____ 被它 ____ 动了.

10. 在旧社会，很多中国人民 ____ 抓，____ 杀. 有的还 ____ 逼
    得卖儿卖女.

11. 我 ____ ____ 喜欢听女高音*独唱*，而且喜欢听民乐*.

12. 那个 ____ 人作了很多 ____ 事 ，所以被抓了.

13. 他连衣服 ____ 没换就出去了.

Change into passive voice:

1. 这个剧感动了劳动人民.

2. 大家把老舍叫作 "人民艺术家".

3. 小张把我的照相机借走了.

4. 这个演员成功的演出把我们都吸引住了.

5. 这个作家还没把他的话剧翻译成法文.

6. 在那个时代，有人不但把爱国青年抓了，而且还杀了.

7. 他不但把我的自行车借走了，而且把我的汽车也开走了.

8. 坏人连孩子也杀了.

9. 风把报纸都刮走了.

10. 除了小王以外，我谁都请了.

Change the sentences into 连...也 construction with the under-
lined phrases as the focus of the structures. For example:

我没有喝<u>茶</u>就走了.
我连茶也没有喝就走了.

1. <u>那个坏人</u>被这个话剧感动了.

2. <u>那个坏作品</u>让人借走了.

3. 我把<u>我爸爸给我的十元钱</u>化了.

4. 没有钱的人不但没有吃的，穿的，而且被逼得把<u>儿女</u>卖了.

5. 他没吃完<u>饭</u>就走了.

Complete the following sentences:

1. 不但中国人过年的时候要团聚，而且 _____.

2. 这儿的冬天不但雪下得很多，而且 _____.

3. 我不但把功课作完了，而且连 _____.

4. 那个音乐会不但有合唱*，独唱*，而且 _____.

5. 他不常看话剧，连 _____.

Translate into Chinese:

1. Lao She was one of the most famous writers in China.

2. What this writer wrote about was conditions in the Old Society.

3. The synopsis of this play has yet been translated into English.

4. The audience was enchanted by the language of the play.

5. Not only were the patriots arrested and killed, but the poor were forced to work.

6. This novel not only enhanced my knowledge of the Chinese history but also deepened my understanding of the Chinese people.

7. We not only read his works but also translated them into other languages.

8. Even the actor was moved by his own successful performance.

9. The delegation stayed in Beijing for a short time. They did not even visit Yi-He-Yuan (the Summer Palace).

10. Not only have the students not been to a tea house, but not even their teacher has been to one.

Fill in blanks with appropriate vocabulary.

1. 这位有名的作家的作品，有的我看过，____ ____ 我没看过.

2. 今年我是在中国过 ____ 春节.

3. 这家饭馆的小吃，____ 好吃又便宜.

4. ____ ____ 外边天气太冷了，所以我们昨晚没出去.

5. ____ ____ 这位伟大的艺术家逝世了，但是大家还是怀念着他.

6. 青年们都 ____ 鲁迅看作自己的好朋友，好老师.

7. 我一看见她 ____ 觉得她像我的姐姐.

8. 你要是今天不太忙，____ 请到我家来坐坐.

9. 只有不太忙的时候我 ____ 能到外边走走.

10. 除了游泳 ____ ____，他们 ____ 钓鱼了.

11. 谁 ____ 大家叫作 "人民艺术家"?

12. 这位艺术家 ____ ____ 在中国很有名，而且在世界上也很有名.

13. 谁 ____ 会被这儿的风景吸引住.

14. ____ ____ 风雪很大，但是梅花还是挺立着.

15. 太热了，请你 ____ 窗户打开.

16. 我们都去参观那个画展了，连老师 ____ 去了.

17. 这个学生不很聪明，____ 不用功.

18. 他每天 ____ 到十二点就睡觉了.

19. ____ ____ 每天练习说汉语，汉语才能说得很流利.

20. ____ ____ 每天练习说汉语，汉语就能说得很流利.

Complete the following sentences:

1. 花儿被

2. 我把钱

3. 他们是上星期六

4. 礼堂里边

5. 因为我们认识的时间不长，

6. 我们一到公园

7. 除了小张以外，

8. 要是

9. 只有

10. 不但

11. 虽然

12. 观众都被这个剧吸引住了，连

Translate into Chinese:

1. It was in 1976 that the premier passed away.

2. Only when one writes characters stroke by stroke can one write them beautifully.

3. Last Sunday was their twentieth wedding anniversary.

4. We read his diary page by page.

5. This painter was one of the greatest artists in the world.

6. The guide at the art gallery said with smile, "Your comments, please."

7. The one who attracted our attention most was a little girl of six or seven (years old).

8. The students came out from the auditorium one by one. The last one was a boy of thirteen (years old).

Appendix I

Character	Pinyin	English	Lesson
		a	
阿姨	āyí	auntie	39
爱	ài	to love	45
		b	
把	bǎ	a preposition	46
把	bǎ	a measure word	47
百	bǎi	hundred	33
摆	bǎi	to put; to lay （the table）	48
百货大楼	Bǎihuò Dàlóu	The （Beijing）Department Store	36
拜年	bàinián	pay a New Year call; wish somebody a happy New Year	48
搬	bān	to move; to take away	42
班	bān	class; squad	42
办公室	bàngōngshì	office	42
包	bāo	to wrap; to make （dumplings）	48
包裹	bāoguǒ	parcel	39
薄	báo	thin	34
保持	bǎochí	to keep/retain	40
爆竹	bàozhú	firecracker	48
北边	běibiān	north; northern part	47
北海	Běihǎi	Beihai Park	32
北京动物园	Běijīng Dòngwùyuán	the Beijing Zoo	45
北京语言学院	Běijīng YǔYán Xuéyuàn	Beijing Languages Institute	31
被	bèi	a preposition	49
本	běn	this; one's own; native	34
本子	běnzi	book; notebook	39
逼	bī	to force; to compel	32
鼻子	bízi	nose	32
笔	bǐ	a measure word	50
比较	bǐjiào	comparatively; quite; to compare	43
毕业	bìyè	to graduate	44
边	biān	side; edge （of a lake, etc.）	44

遍	biàn	a measure word	32
表	biǎo	form（telegraph forms, etc.）	32
表	biǎo	（wrist）watch	35
别的	biéde	other; another	43
别人	biérén	other people; others	36
冰棍儿	bīnggùnr	ice-lolly; ice-sucker	42
病	bìng	to be ill; illness	32
病房	bìngfáng	ward（of a hospital）	46
病人	bìngrén	patient	46
不但…而且…	búdàn…érqiě…	not only … but also …	49
布	bù	cotton cloth	34
不好意思	bù hǎoyìsi	to feel embarrassed; to feel embarrassing（to do something）	39
布鞋	bùxié	cloth shoes	37
不用	búyòng	there is no need to	31

c/ch

才	cái	only; just; not…until	41
彩旗	cǎiqí	colored flag	40
菜单	càidān	menu	43
操场	cāochǎng	sportsground	40
草	cǎo	grass	44
茶馆	cháguǎn	teahouse	49
茶壶	cháhú	teapot	36
茶具	chájù	tea set; tea service	36
茶碗	cháwǎn	teacup	36
长	cháng	long	31
长城	Chángchéng	The Great Wall	32
长廊	Cháng Láng	Long Corridor	44
长短	chángduǎn	length	37
车间	chējiān	workshop	39
陈毅	Chén Yì	Chen Yi	33
成	chéng	to become; to turn into	47
成功	chénggōng	to succeed	49
成绩	chéngjì	result; achievement	35
尺	chǐ	ruler	42
崇祯	Chóngzhēn	Emperor Chongzhen	41
绸子	chóuzi	silk fabric	37
出	chū	to come out; to go out	31
初	chū	a prefix	48

出差	chūchāi	to be away on official business; be on a business trip	44
出院	chūyuàn	to leave hospital	47
出租汽车	chūzūqìchē	taxi; cab	38
除了...以外	chúle...yǐwài	besides; except	47
除夕	chúxī	New Year's Eve	48
穿（马路）	chuān（mǎlù）	to cross（a street）	43
船	chuán	boat	44
窗户	chuānghu	window	44
窗口	chuāngkǒu	window	34
春节	chūnjié	Spring Festival	48
春联	chūnlián	Spring Festival couplets; New Year scrolls	48
春天	chūntiān	spring	39
瓷器	cíqì	chinaware; porcelain	36
次	cì	a measure word; time	31
聪明	cōngming	intelligent; bright	39
存车处	cúnchēchù	parking lot（for bicycles）	43
错	cuò	wrong	38
错误	cuòwù	mistake	47

d

达尼亚	Dáníyà	name of a person	44
打（拳）	dǎ（quán）	to do shadowboxing	40
打（针）	dǎ（zhēn）	to give/have an injection	46
打开	dǎkāi	to open	50
打破	dǎpò	to break	40
打扫	dǎsǎo	to clean up	48
大便	dàbiàn	stool; human excrement	46
大闹天宫	Dànàotiāngōng	"The Monkey Creates Havoc in Heaven"	32
大娘	dàniáng	aunt	38
大声	dàshēng	in loud voice; loudly	34
大学	dàxué	university; college	31
大爷	dàyé	uncle	38
带	dài	to take（along）; to bring（with）	38
戴	dài	to wear（e.g. cap, glasses, gloves）	45
袋	dài	bag; sack	48
单	dān	bill; list; form	34
但是	dànshì	but	39
当心	dāngxīn	to take care; to look out	43
得（病）	dé（bìng）	to fall ill; to contract a disease	32

地	de	a structural particle	34
灯	dēng	lantern; lamp; light	48
灯节	dēngjié	the Lantern Festival（15th of the 1st month of the lunar calendar）	48
灯笼	dēnglóng	lantern	48
第	dì	a prefix indicating order	31
地方	dìfang	place	32
地铁	dìtiě	the underground; subway	38
典型	diǎnxíng	typical; model	42
店	diàn	shop; store	43
电报	diànbào	telegram; cable	34
电车	diànchē	trolleybus	38
吊	diào	to hang	41
订	dìng	to subscribe to（a newspaper, etc.）	36
定作	dìngzuò	to have something made; to order	37
丢	diū	to lose	41
东边	dōngbiān	east; eastern part	38
东西	dōngxi	thing	30
动	dòng	to move	42
动物	dòngwù	animal	45
动物园	dòngwùyuán	zoo	45
豆腐	dòufu	bean curd	43
独唱	dúchàng	solo; to solo	43
度	dù	a measure word, degree	33
度假	dùjià	to spend one's holidays	44
短	duǎn	short	37
对	duì	to; for	39
对不起	duìbuqǐ	（I'm）sorry	41
对象	duìxiàng	boy or girl friend	44
多么	duōme	how; what	44

e

饿	è	to be hungry; hungry	43
儿子	érzi	son	48
耳朵	ěrduo	ear	32

f

发烧	fāshāo	to have a fever	46
发展	fāzhǎn	to develop	36

饭馆	fànguǎn	restaurant	43
方便	fāngbiàn	convenient; to make it convenient for	42
方向	fāngxiàng	direction	38
放	fàng	to put; to place	34
放（爆竹）	fàng（bàozhú）	to let off（firecrackers）	48
放（假）	fàng（jià）	to have a holiday or vacation	35
非洲	Fēizhōu	Africa	45
肥	féi	loose-fitting; fat	37
肺	fèi	lungs	32
肺炎	fèiyán	pneumonia	32
分	fēn	a measure word（the smallest Chinese monetary unit）	36
风	fēng	wind	33
封	fēng	a measure word	34
丰富	fēngfù	rich; abundant; to enrich	47
风景	fēngjǐng	scenery; landscape	44
风俗	fēngsú	custom	48
风味	fēngwèi	local flavor; local style	43
服务	fúwù	service; to serve	43
幅	fú	a measure word	44
阜城门	Fùchéngmén	name of a place in Beijing	47

g

改	gǎi	to correct	47
盖儿	gàir	cover; lid	42
肝	gān	liver	32
乾净	gānjjing	clean; neat and tidy	48
感动	gǎndong	to move; to touch; moving	49
感冒	gǎnmào	to catch cold;（common）cold	46
感想	gǎnxiǎng	impressions; feeling	47
干	gàn	to work; to do	42
刚	gāng	just; only a short while ago	38
钢铁学院	Gāngtiě Xuéyuàn	The Beijing Iron & Steel Engineering Institute	38
高	gāo	tall	37
各	gè	each; every; various; respectively	43
个子	gèzi	height; stature; build	32
工地	gōngdì	construction site	42
公分	gōngfēn	a measure word, centimeter	37
公共	gōnggòng	public	38

公共汽车	gōnggòngqìchē	bus	38
恭贺新禧	gōnghèxīnxǐ	Happy New Year	48
公斤	gōngjīn	kilogram （kg.）	42
公园	gōngyuán	park	33
够	gòu	enough; sufficient	43
古	gǔ	ancient	33
鼓掌	gǔzhǎng	to applaud	40
故宫	gùgōng	the Imperial Palace	41
故居	gùjū	former residence	47
顾客	gùkè	customer	43
故事	gùshì	story	38
顾问	gùwèn	adviser	42
刮（风）	guā（fēng）	to blow （said of wind）	35
挂	guà	to hang; to put up	34
挂号	guàhào	to register （a letter, etc.）	34
挂号证	guàhàozhèng	register card	46
拐弯	guǎiwuān	to turn a corner	38
关	guān	to close; to shut	46
关心	guānxīn	to care for; to be concerned with	39
观众	guānzhòng	spectator; audience	40
广播	guǎngbō	to broadcast	40
广播室	guǎngbōshì	broadcasting room	41
广播员	guǎngbōyuán	radio （or wire-broadcasting）announcer	41
广场	guǎngcháng	spuare	41
广州	Guǎngzhōu	name of a city	44
贵	guì	expensive	36
柜台	guìtái	counter	34
国际	guójì	international	31
过	guò	to come over; to pass by	41
过	guò	a structural particle	32

h

海	hǎi	sea	50
寒假	hánjià	winter vacation	35
喊	hǎn	to shout	44
航空	hángkōng	air （mail）	34
好吃	hǎochī	delicious; tasty	43
合唱	héchàng	chorus; to chorus	49
合适	héshì	suitable, fit	37
黑暗	hēi'àn	dark	49

红莲	hónglián	red lotus	50
红绿灯	hónglǜdēng	(red & green) traffic light	38
红叶	hóngyè	red autumnal leaves (of maple, etc.)	33
厚	hòu	thick	36
后来	hòulái	afterwards; later	45
壶	hú	pot, a measure word	36
湖	hú	lake	44
胡同	hútòng	lane; alley	38
护士	hùshì	nurse	46
护照	hùzhào	passport	31
花	huā	to spend (money)	37
华表	huábiǎo	marble pillar (an ornamental column erected in front of palaces, tombs, etc.)	42
华侨	huáqiáo	overseas Chinese	31
话	huà	words; talk	31
画	huà	to paint, to draw	36
画儿	huàr	picture; painting	36
话剧	huàjù	spoken drama	49
画蛇添足	huàshétiānzú	(fig.) ruin the effect by adding what is superfluous	36
画展	huàzhǎn	art exhibition	50
怀念	huáiniàn	to cherish the memory of; to think of	47
坏	huài	bad; there is somthing wrong with	49
欢迎	huānyíng	to welcome	49
换	huàn	to change	38
黄	huáng	a surname	48
皇帝	huángdì	emperor	41
灰	huī	grey	37
恢复	huīfù	to recover	47
活	huó	to live; alive; living	47
活儿	huór	work; job	42
货	huò	goods; commodity	36

j

迹	jī	trace; track; sign	33
激动	jīdòng	excited	40
机会	jīhuì	chance; opportunity	35
...极了	jíle	extremely; exceedingly	40
挤	jǐ	crowded; to squeeze	41
寄	jì	to post; to mail	34

记	jì	to remember; to bear in mind	39
记录	jìlù	record	40
纪念	jìniàn	to commemorate; commemoration	47
假期	jiàqī	vacation	35
价钱	jiàqián	price	36
间	jiān	a measure word	47
检查	jiǎnchá	check up; physical examination	32
简朴	jiǎnpǔ	simple and unadorned	47
建设	jiànshè	to build; to construct; construction	31
建筑	jiànzhù	building; to build; to construct	41
江西	Jiāngxī	name of a Chinese province	36
讲	jiǎng	tell; speak; explain (text, etc.)	38
讲解	jiǎngjié	to explain	47
讲解员	jiǎngjiéyuán	guide	47
奖状	jiǎngzhuàng	certificate of merit	42
交	jiāo	to pay (money)	37
脚	jiǎo	foot	41
饺子	jiǎozi	dumpling	46
叫	jiào	a preposition	49
街	jiē	street	38
接	jiē	to extend; to connect	47
街道	jiēdào	street	39
节	jié	festival	48
节目	jiémù	programme; item	49
节日	jiérì	festival; holiday	48
解	jiě	to relieve oneself	46
解放	jiěfàng	to liberate	36
借	jiè	to borrow; to lend	49
近	jìn	near	44
景德镇	Jǐngdézhèn	name of a Chinese city	36
景山	Jǐngshān	name of a hill in Jingshan park	41
景山公园	Jǐngshān Gōngyuán	name of a park in Beijng	41
镜头	jìngtóu	camera lens	42
镜子	jìngzi	mirror	44
句	jù	a measure word, for sentences or lines of verse	39
剧场	jùchǎng	theatre	49
绝	jué	disappear, vanish; by no means	33
觉得	juéde	to think; to feel	33
决定	juédìng	to decide; decision	44

k

开会	kāihuì	to hold or attend a meeting	31
开学	kāixué	school opens; new term begins	35
开演	kāiyǎn	(of a play, movie, etc.) to begin	49
看（病）	kàn (bìng)	to see (a doctor, etc.)	35
考	kǎo	to test	35
考试	kǎoshì	to test; examination	35
科	kē	department (of internal medicine, etc.)	46
咳嗽	késou	to cough	46
渴	kě	thirsty	43
可爱	kě'ài	lovely	45
可能	kěnéng	may; probable; possible	46
可笑	kěxiào	funny; rediculous	45
客人	kèren	guest; visitor	39
块（元）	kuài (yuán)	a measure word (a Chinese monetary unit, equal to 10 jiao or mao)	36
宽	kuān	wide	42
昆明湖	Kūnmíng Hú	Kunming Lake	44

l

拉	lā	to play (string instruments)	31
蓝	lán	blue	37
兰花	lánhuā	cymbidium; orchid	50
劳动	láodòng	to labor; to work	49
老	lǎo	old; aged	31
老虎	lǎohǔ	tiger	47
老骥伏枥，志在千里	lǎojìfúlì zhìzàiqiānlǐ	an old steed in the stable still aspires to gallop a thousand li; (fig.) old people may still cherish high aspirations	39
姥姥	lǎolao	maternal grandmother, grandma	46
老舍	lǎoshě	name of a person	49
累	lèi	to feel tired	43
冷	lěng	cold	33
礼堂	lǐtáng	assembly hall; auditorium	42
礼物	lǐwù	gift; present	48
李自成	Lǐ Zìchéng	name of a person	41
立	lì	to stand; to erect	33
厉害	lìhai	serious; terrible	46
立刻	lìkè	immediately; at once	46

丽丽	lìlì	name of a person	45
历史	lìshǐ	history	36
利用	lìyòng	to use; to make use of	35
连…也…	lián…yě…	even	19
量	liáng	to measure	32
凉快	liángkuai	nice and cold; pleasantly cool	33
粮食	liángshí	grain; food	48
辆	liàng	a measure word for vehicles	37
亮	liàng	light; bright	43
了	liǎo	to end up	42
料子	liàozi	material	37
邻居	línjú	neighbor	39
临摹	línmó	to copy（a model of calligraphy or painting, etc.）	50
零	líng	zero	36
零钱	língqián	change（said of money）	36
留	liú	remain; ask somebody to stay	39
留言	liúyán	leave one's comments or a message	47
留言簿	liúyánbù	visitors' book	47
隆冬	lóngdōng	midwinter; the depth of winter	33
路	lù	road; way	31
路口	lùkǒu	crossing; intersection	38
录音	lùyīn	to record; recording	46
旅馆	lǚguǎn	hotel	41
旅行	lǚxíng	to travel	44
绿灯	lǜdēng	green light	43
骆驼祥子	Luòtuó Xiángzǐ	name of a novel	49

m

麻烦	máfan	to bother; troublesome	48
马	mǎ	horse	38
马路	mǎlù	road; street	38
卖	mài	to sell	49
毛衣	máoyī	woollen sweater	37
毛主席	Máo Zhǔxí	Chairman Mao	42
贸易	màoyì	trade	44
没关系	méiguānxi	it doesn't matter	41
梅花	méihuā	plum blossom	33
美	měi	beautiful	41
美国	Měiguó	the United States（of America）	31

门口	ménkǒu	doorway; entrance	41
米	mǐ	a measure word, meter	37
棉袄	mián'ǎo	cotton-padded jacket	37
面儿	miànr	cover; outside	37
秒	miǎo	a measure word, second	40
民乐	mínyuè	music; esp. folk music, for traditional instruments	49
名	míng	a measure word	40
明信片	míngxìnpiàn	postcard	34
摩托车	mótuōchē	motorcycle	41
墨镜	mòjìng	sunglasses	45
母亲	mǔqin	mother	44

n

拿	ná	to get; to take	32
南边	nánbiān	south; southern part	38
南京	Nánjīng	Nanjing (city)	34
南亚	Nán Yà	South Asia	45
南辕北辙	nányuánběizhé	(fig.) act in a way that defeats one's purpose	38
男子	nánzǐ	man	40
内科	nèikē	medical department	32
年	nián	New Year	48
年画儿	niánhuàr	New Year (or Spring Festival) picture	48
年夜饭	niányèfàn	New Year's Eve family dinner	48
牛	niú	ox; cattle	47
牛奶	niúnǎi	milk	43
女高音	nǚgāoyīn	soprano	49
暖和	nuǎnhuo	warm; nice and warm	33

p

爬	pá	to climb	44
怕	pà	to be afraid; to fear	33
排队	páiduì	to line up	38
牌子	páizi	sign; plate	34
彷徨	Pánghuáng	name of a collection of short stories	47
胖	pàng	fat; stout; plump	37
跑	pǎo	to run	38
培养	péiyǎng	to foster; to bring up	47
篇	piān	a measure word	47

便宜	piányi	cheap	36
片	piàn	a measure word, tablets	46
平安里	Píng'ānlǐ	name of a street in Beijing	38
平方米	píngfāngmǐ	square meter	42
平信	píngxìn	ordinary mail	34

q

骑	qí	to ride （a bicycle）	37
齐白石	Qí Báishí	name of a person	36
奇怪	qíguài	surprised; strange	35
旗袍	qípáo	Chinese-style frock	37
旗子	qízi	flag; banner	40
汽车	qìchē	automobile; car	38
千	qiān	thousand	42
钱	qián	money	35
墙	qiáng	wall	34
敲	qiāo	to knock （at a door）	33
桥	qiáo	bridge	44
亲爱	qīn'ài	dear	48
亲切	qīnqiè	cordial; kind	43
青	qīng	green	44
清楚	qīngchu	clear	41
青年	qīngnián	youth	47
晴	qíng	（of weather）fine; bright; clear	33
情况	qíngkuàng	condition; situation; state of affairs	35
屈服	qūfú	to surrender; to yield	33
全	quán	whole	48
群众	qúnzhòng	mass; people	47

r

让	ràng	a preposition	49
热	rè	hot	33
热烈	rèliè	warm; enthusiastic	40
人民大会堂	Rénmín Dàhuìtáng	Great Hall of the People	42
人民英雄纪念碑	Rénmín Yīngxióng Jìniànbēi	Monument to the People's Heroes	42
人物	rénwù	figure; characters （in a play, etc.）	44
日记	rìjì	diary	49

三国演义	Sānguóyǎnyì	name of a novel, "Romance of the Three Kingdoms"	44
三里河	Sānlǐhé	name of a street in Beijing	38
三里屯	Sānlǐtún	name of a street in Beijing	38
扫	sǎo	to sweep	48
杀	shā	to kill	49
山	shān	hill; mountain	41
上（次）	shàng（cǐ）	last（time）; a previous（occasion）	37
上海	Shànghǎi	Shanghai	31
社会	shèhuì	society	49
社会主义	shèhuìzhǔyì	socialism	31
设计	shèjì	to design	47
生	shēng	to be born	44
生产	shēngchǎn	to produce; to manufacture	36
生活	shēnghuó	life; to live	47
生命	shēngmìng	life	32
圣诞节	shèngdànjié	Christmas Day	48
诗	shī	poem; poetry; verse	33
师傅	shīfu	master worker	43
狮子	shīzi	lion	42
石（头）	shí（tou）	stone; rock	42
时间	shíjiān	（duration of）time;（a point of）time	31
实现	shíxiàn	to realize; to achieve	31
使者	shǐzhě	emissary; envoy	45
市	shì	city	34
世界	shìjiè	the world	50
逝世	shìshì	to pass away	50
收	shōu	to receive	34
收据	shōujù	receipt	34
收拾	shōushi	to put in order; to tidy up	48
收音机	shōuyīnjī	radio	34
首	shǒu	a measure word	33
手	shǒu	hand	46
首都	shǒudū	capital of a country	31
首都国际机场	Shǒudū Guójì Jīchǎng	the Capital International Airprot, Beijing	31
首都剧场	Shǒudū Jùchǎng	the Capital Theatre	49
手续	shǒuxù	formalities	31

瘦	shòu	tight; thin; lean	37
售货员	shòuhuòyuán	shop assistant	36
售票处	shòupiàochù	ticket office; booking office	41
售票员	shòupiàoyuán	ticket seller; conductor	38
舒服	shūfu	comfortable; well	46
书架	shūjià	bookshelf	39
叔叔	shūshu	father's younger brother; uncle	39
暑假	shǔjià	summer vacation	35
树	shù	tree	33
说明书	shuōmíngshū	synopsis（of a play or film）	49
司机	sījī	driver	41
死	sǐ	to die	41
虽然	suīrán	though; although	39
岁数	suìshu	age	42
所以	suǒyǐ	so; therefore; as a result	44

t

它	tā	it	44
它们	tāmen	they（refers to things, animals）	45
塔	tǎ	pagoda	44
太极拳	tàijíquán	a kind of traditional Chinese shadowboxing	40
太阳	tàiyáng	the sun	44
探亲	tànqīn	to go home to visit one's family	44
糖	táng	sugar	43
唐山	Tángshān	name of a city	36
躺	tǎng	to lie	36
套	tào	a measure word, set	36
疼	téng	ache; pain; sore	46
藤野	Téngyě	name of a person	47
提	tí	to suggest; to put forward	43
提高	tígāo	to increase; to improve	36
体温	tǐwēn	（body）temperature	46
天	tiān	sky; heaven	44
天安门	Tiān'ānmén	Tian'anmen（Gate of Heavenly Peace）	34
天安门广场	Tiān'ānmén Guǎngchǎng	Tiananmen Square	41
天气	tiānqì	weather	31
填	tián	to fill	32
条子	tiáozi	a short note; a slip of paper	39

跳	tiào	to jump	44
贴	tiē	to paste	48
听说	tīngshuō	it is said that	41
挺立	tǐnglì	to stand erect; to stand upright	50
亭子	tíngzi	pavilion	41
同志	tóngzhì	comrade	31
头	tóu	head	45
头发	tóufa	hair（on human head）	32
透视	tòushì	to examine by fluoroscope; to take X-ray examination	32
图片	túpiàn	picture; photograph	34
兔子	tùzi	hare; rabbit	48
团聚	tuánjù	to reunite; to have a reunion	48
推	tuī	to push	43
腿	tuǐ	leg	45
退休	tuìxiū	to retire	39

W

袜子	wàzi	socks; stockings	37
外国	wàiguó	foreign country	45
豌豆赵	Wāndòu Zhào	name of a person	43
豌豆粥	wāndòu zhōu	pea gruel	43
完	wán	to finish; to be over	39
完成	wánchéng	to complete; to finish	42
碗	wǎn	bowl; a measure word, bowl	36
万	wàn	ten thousand	42
万寿山	Wànshòu Shān	Longevity Hill	44
往	wǎng	to go（to a place）	38
往	wàng	toward;（train）bound for	33
微笑	wēixiào	to smile	50
尾巴	wěiba	tail	47
伟大	wěida	great	47
胃	wèi	stomach	32
为甚麽	wèi shénme	why	34
文学家	wénxuéjiā	writer; man of letters	47
文章	wénzhāng	writings	47
屋子	wūzi	room	48
舞蹈	wǔdǎo	dance	49
雾	wù	fog; mist	33

西边	xībiān	west; western part	41
西三条	Xīsāntiáo	name of a place in Beijing	47
希望	xīwàng	to hope; to wish; hope; wish	31
吸引	xīyǐn	to attrack; to draw	49
西装	xīzhuāng	Western-style suit	37
习惯	xíguàn	to be used to; to be accustomed to; habit; custom	33
洗	xǐ	to wash	41
洗（照片）	xǐ（zhàopiàn）	to develope（a film）	42
下	xià	to get off（bus, etc）	38
下（星期）	xià（xīngqī）	next（week）	37
下（雨）	xià（yǔ）	to rain	33
下边	xiàbiān	below; under; underneath	34
夏历	xiàlì	the traditional Chinese calendar	48
先	xiān	first	32
现代化	xiàndàihuà	modernization	31
香山	Xiāng Shān	Fragrance Hill（Park）	33
象	xiàng	elephant	45
向导	xiàngdǎo	guide	41
小吃	xiǎochī	snack; refreshments	43
小吃店	xiǎochīdiàn	snack bar; lunch room	43
小冬	Xiǎodōng	name of a child	42
小红	Xiǎohóng	name of a child	42
小兰	Xiǎolán	name of a person	39
小声	xiǎoshēng	in a low voice;（speak）in whispers	46
小时	xiǎoshí	hour	31
小说	xiǎoshuō	novel; short story	41
小提琴	xiǎotíqín	violin	31
辛苦	xīnkǔ	hard; exhausting; with much toil	31
新年	xīnnián	new year	48
心臓	xīnzàng	heart	32
信封	xìnfēng	envelope	34
信箱	xìnxiāng	post-office box（P.O.B.）; letter box; mail box	34
姓名	xìngmíng	full name; surname and given name	34
杏仁	xìngrén	almond	43
杏仁豆腐	xìngréndòufu	almond junket	43
熊猫	xióngmāo	panda	45
熊猫馆	xióngmāoguǎn	panda exhibition hall	45

修	xiū	to build（road, etc）; to repair	38
修建	xiūjiàn	to build; to construct	42
选举	xuǎnjǔ	to elect	39
学期	xuéqī	term; semester	35
学校	xuéxiào	school	31
雪	xuě	snow	33
血	xuè	blood	32
血压	xuèyā	blood pressure	32

y

亚洲	Yà Zhōu	Asia	45
颜色	yánsè	color	37
演	yǎn	to perform; to play; to act	49
演出	yǎnchū	to perform; to put on a show; performance; show	49
眼睛	yǎnjīng	eye	32
演员	yǎnyuán	actor or actress; performer	49
阳阳	Yángyáng	name of a child	48
样子	yàngzi	manner; air; looks	45
药	yào	medicine	46
要不	yàobù	or; or else; otherwise	37
药方	yàofāng	prescription	46
药剂士	yàojìshì	druggist; pharmacist	46
要是	yàoshì	if	41
爷爷	yéye	grandpa	42
野草	yěcǎo	name of a collection of prose poems	47
页	yè	page; a measure word, page	50
叶子	yèzi	leaf	33
衣服	yīfu	clothes; clothing	37
衣柜	yīguì	wardrobe	39
一…就…	yì…jiù…	no sooner than; as soon as	39
医务所	yīwùsuǒ	clinic	32
医院	yīyuàn	hospital	46
遗产	yíchǎn	heritage	47
一共	yígòng	altogether; in all	36
颐和园	Yíhéyuán	Summer Palace	33
一会儿	yíhuìr	a little while	41
一样	yíyàng	same; identical	37
已经	yǐjīng	already	31
以前	yǐqián	before; in the past	32

意见	yìjiàn	criticism; comment or suggestions	43
艺术	yìshù	art	42
艺术家	yìshùjiā	artist	49
意思	yìsi	meaning	39
阴天	yīntiān	cloudy day; overcast sky	33
因为	yīnwèi	because; for	48
迎春花	yíngchūnhuā	winter jasmine	50
营业	yíngyè	to do business	34
营业员	yíngyèyuán	clerk; shop assistant	34
永远	yǒngyuǎn	always; forever	39
油饼	yóubǐng	deep-fried pancake	43
邮局	yóujú	post office	34
邮票	yóupiào	stamp	34
有的	yǒude	some	34
有（一）点儿	yǒu（yì）diǎnr	a bit	43
愉快	yúkuài	happy; delighted	39
雨	yǔ	rain	33
语言	yǔyán	language	31
雨衣	yǔyī	raincoat	37
玉	yù	jade	36
预报	yùbào	forecast	33
园林	yuánlín	gardens; park; landscape garden	44
元宵	yuánxiāo	sweet dumplings made of glutinous rice flour	43
元宵节	Yuánxiāo Jié	the Lantern Festival	48
远方	yuǎnfāng	distant place	39
院子	yuànzi	courtyard	47
运动	yùndòng	to exercise （oneself）; sport	40
运动会	yùndònghuì	sports meet	40
运动员	yùndòngyuán	sportsman; player	40

z/zh

咱们	zánmen	we	38
枣树	zǎoshù	jujube tree; date tree	47
怎麽	zěnme	how; why	38
炸糕	zhágāo	fried cake	43
站	zhàn	stop	38
张华光	Zhāng Huáguāng	name of a person	31
张华明	Zhāng Huámíng	name of a person	41

掌柜	zhǎngguì	shopkeeper	49
著急	zháojí	feel anxiously	35
找（钱）	zhǎo（qián）	to give change	36
照相机	zhàoxiàngjī	camera	41
这麼	zhème	so; such	42
这样	zhèyàng	so; such; like this	32
著	zhe	a particle	34
针	zhēn	injection; needle	46
珍贵	zhēnguì	precious; valuable	45
整齐	zhěngqí	neat; tidy	48
挣	zhèng	to earn; to make（money）	35
正常	zhèngcháng	normal; regular	32
正确	zhèngquè	correct; right	49
之	zhī	a modal particle; a pronoun	43
只	zhī	a measure word	45
枝	zhī	a measure word	50
知识	zhīshì	knowledge	32
...之一	...zhīyī	one of ...	49
指	zhǐ	to point at; to point to	34
只	zhǐ	only	36
只有	zhǐyǒu	only	44
质量	zhìliàng	quality	36
钟	zhōng	clock	31
终点	zhōngdiǎn	terminal point; terminus	38
中国历史博物馆	Zhōngguó Lìshǐ Bówùguǎn	Museum of Chinese History	42
中国美术馆	Zhōngguó Měishù Guǎn	National Art Gallery	50
中间	zhōngjiān	center; middle	42
中山装	zhōngshānzhuāng	Chinese tunic suit	37
中式	zhōngshì	Chinese style	37
种	zhǒng	a measure word, kind; type	36
重	zhòng	heavy	42
种	zhòng	to grow; to plant	46
粥	zhōu	gruel; porridge	43
周到	zhōudào	thoughtful; considerate	41
周恩来	Zhōu Ēnlái	Zhou Enlai	50
周年	zhōunián	anniversary	50
周总理	Zhōu Zǒnglǐ	Premier Zhou	50
株	zhū	a measure word	47

竹（子）	zhú（zi）	bamboo	45
主任	zhǔrèn	director; head	39
主席	zhǔxí	chairman	40
主席台	zhǔxítaí	rostrum; platform	40
住院	zhùyuàn	to be in hospital; to be hospitalized	46
抓	zhuā	to arrest; to catch; to clutch	49
专业	zhuānyè	specialty; specialized suject	35
自行车	zìxíngchē	bicycle; bike	36
总理	zǒnglǐ	premier	50
嘴	zuǐ	mouth	32
最	zuì	best; most; least; to the highest （lowest）degree	33
最	zuìhòu	last	50
最近	zuìjìn	recently; lately	32
作	zuò	to regard as; to take （somebody）for	47
座	zuò	a measure word	44
作品	zuòpǐn	works （of literature and art）	49
座位	zuòwèi	seat	38

APPENDIX II

English	Pinyin	Character	Lesson
		a	
a bit	yǒu (yì) diǎr	有（一）点儿	43
a little while	yíhuìr	一会儿	41
abundant	fēngfù	丰富	47
ache	téng	疼	46
achieve	shíxiàn	实现	31
achievement	chéngjī	成绩	35
act (e.g. in movies)	yǎn	演	37
act in a way that defeats one's purpose （fig.）	nányuánběizhé	南辕北辙	38
actor/actress	yǎnyuán	演员	49
adviser	gùwèn	顾问	42
Africa	Fēizhōu	非洲	45
afterwards	hòulái	后来	45
age	suìshu	岁数	42
aged	lǎo	老	31
air （one's bearings）	yàngzi	样子	45
air （mail）	hángkōng	航空	34
alley	hútòng	胡同	38
almond	xìngrén	杏仁	43
almond junket	xìngréndòufu	杏仁豆腐	43
already	yǐjīng	已经	31
although	suīrán	虽然	39
altogether	yígòng	一共	36
always	yǒngyuǎn	永远	39
ancient	gǔ	古	33
animal	dòngwù	动物	45
anniversary	zhōunián	周年	50
another	biéde	别的	43
applaud	gǔzhǎng	鼓掌	40
arrest	zhuā	抓	49
art	yìshù	艺术	42
art exhibition	huàzhǎn	画展	50
artist	yìshùjiā	艺术家	49
as a result	suǒyi	所以	44
as soon as	yī…jiù…	一…就…	39

Asia	Yà Zhōu	亚洲	45
ask somebody to stay	liú	留	39
assembly hall	lǐtáng	礼堂	42
at once	lìkè	立刻	46
athlete	yùndòngyuán	运动员	40
attend a meeting	kāihuì	开会	31
attrack	xiyǐn	吸引	49
audience	guānzhòng	观众	40
auditorium	lǐtáng	礼堂	42
aunt	dàniáng	大娘	38
auntie	āyí	阿姨	39
automobile	qìchē	汽车	38

b

bad	huài	坏	49
bag	dài	袋	48
bamboo	zhú（zi）	竹（子）	45
banner	qízi	旗子	40
be accustomed to	xíguàn	习惯	37
be afraid	pà	怕	33
be away on official business	chūchāi	出差	44
be born	shēng	生	44
be concerned with	guānxīn	关心	39
be hospitalized, in hospital	zhùyuàn	住院	46
be on a business trip	chūchāi	出差	44
be over	wán	完	39
be used to	xíguàn	习惯	37
bean curd	dòufu	豆腐	43
bear in mind	jì	记	39
beautiful	měi	美	41
because	yīnwèi	因为	48
become	chéng	成	47
before	yǐqián	以前	32
begin（of play/movie）	kāiyǎn	开演	49
Beihai Park	Běihǎi	北海	32
Beijing Iron & Steel Engineering Institute	Gāngtiě Xuéyuàn	钢铁学院	38
Beijing Languages Institute	Běijīng Yǔyán Xuéyuàn	北京语言学院	31

English	Pinyin	Chinese	Page
Beijing Zoo	Běijīng Dòngwùyuán	北京动物园	45
below	xiàbiān	下边	34
besides	chúle...yǐwài	除了...以外	47
best	zuì	最	33
bill	dān	单	34
blood	xuè	血	32
blood preasure	xuèyā	血压	32
blow（said of wind）	guā（fēng）	刮（风）	35
blue	lán	蓝	37
boat	chuán	船	44
body temperature	tǐwēn	体温	46
book	běnzi	本子	39
booking office	shòupiànchù	售票处	41
bookshelf	shūjià	书架	39
borrow	jiè	借	49
bother	máfan	麻烦	48
bound for（said of train）	wàng	往	38
bowl	wǎn	碗	36
bowl（as measure word）	wǎn	碗	36
boy or girl friend	duìxiàng	对象	44
break	dǎpò	打破	40
bridge	qiáo	桥	44
bright	cōngming	聪明	39
bright	liàng	亮	43
bright（weather）	qíng	晴	33
bring up	péiyǎng	培养	47
bring（with）	dài	带	38
broadcast	guǎngbō	广播	40
broadcasting room	guǎngbōshì	广播室	41
build	jiànshè	建设	31
build	jiànzhù	建筑	41
build（road, etc.）	xiū	修	38
build	xiūjiàn	修建	42
building	jiànzhù	建筑	41
bus	gōnggōngqìzhē	公共汽车	38
but	dànshì	但是	39
by no means	jué	绝	33
bicycle/bike	zìxíngchē	自行车	36

c

cab	chūzūqìchē	出租汽车	38
cable	diànbào	电报	34
camera	zhàoxiàngjī	照相机	11
camera lens	jìngtóu	镜头	42
Capital International Airport, Beijing	Shǒudū Guójì Jīchǎng	首都国际机场	31
Capital Theatre	Shǒudū Jùchǎng	首都剧场	49
capital of a country	shǒudū	首都	31
car	qìchē	汽车	38
care for	guānxīn	关心	39
catch	zhuā	抓	49
catch cold	gǎnmào	感冒	46
cattle	niú	牛	47
center	zhōngjiān	中间	42
centimeter	gōngfēn	公分	37
certificate of merit	jiǎngzhuàng	奖状	42
chairman	zhǔxí	主席	40
Chairman Mao	Máo Zhǔxí	毛主席	42
chance	jīhuì	机会	35
change	huàn	换	38
change（said of money）	língqián	零钱	36
characters（in plays/novels）	rénwù	人物	44
cheap	piányi	便宜	36
check up	jiǎnchá	检查	32
Chen Yi	Chén Yì	陈毅	33
cherish the memory of	huáiniàn	怀念	47
chinaware	cíqì	瓷器	36
Chinese style	zhōngshì	中式	37
Chinese-style frock	qípáo	旗袍	37
Chinese tunic suit	zhōngshānzhuāng	中山装	37
chorus	héchàng	合唱	49
Christmas Day	shèngdànjié	圣诞节	48
city	shì	市	34
class	bān	班	42
clean	gānjing	乾净	48
clean up	dǎsǎo	打扫	48
clear	qīngchu	清楚	41
clear（weather）	qíng	晴	33
clerk	yíngyèyuán	营业员	34
climb	pá	爬	44
clinic	yīwùsuǒ	医务所	32

clock	zhōng	钟	31
close	guān	关	46
cloth shoes	bùxié	布鞋	37
clothes	yīfu	衣服	37
clothing	yīfu	衣服	37
cloudy day	yīntiān	阴天	33
clutch	zhuā	抓	49
cold	lěng	冷	33
college	dàxué	大学	31
color	yánsè	颜色	45
colored flag	cǎiqí	彩旗	40
come out	chū	出	31
come over	guò	过	41
comfortable	shūfu	舒服	46
commemorate	jìniàn	纪念	47
commemoration	jìniàn	纪念	47
comment or suggestions	yìjiàn	意见	43
commodity	huò	货	36
common cold	gǎnmào	感冒	46
comparatively	bǐjiào	比较	43
compare	bǐjiào	比较	43
compel	bī	逼	32
complete	wánchéng	完成	42
comrade	tóngzhì	同志	31
condition	qíngkuàng	情况	35
conductor (on bus)	shòupiàoyuán	售票员	41
connect	jiē	接	47
considerate	zhōudào	周到	41
construct	xiūjiàn	修建	42
construct	jiànshè	建设	31
construct	jiànzhù	建筑	41
construction	jiànshè	建设	31
construction site	gōngdì	工地	42
contract a disease	dé (bìng)	得（病）	32
convenient	fāngbiàn	方便	42
copy （a model of calligraphy/painting）	línmó	临摹	50
cordial	qīnqiè	亲切	43
correct	zhèngquè	正确	49
correct something	gǎi	改	47
cotton cloth	bù	布	34

cotton-padded jacket	mián'ǎo	棉袄	37
cough	késou	咳嗽	46
counter	guìtái	柜台	34
courtyard	yuànzi	院子	47
cover	miànr	面儿	37
cover	gàir	盖儿	42
criticism	yìjiàn	意见	43
cross （a street）	chuān （mǎlù）	穿（马路）	43
crossing	lùkǒu	路口	38
crowded	jǐ	挤	41
custom	fēngsú	风俗	48
custom	xíguàn	习惯	37
customer	gùkè	顾客	43
cymbidium	lánhuā	兰花	50

d

dance	wǔdǎo	舞蹈	49
dark	hēi'àn	黑暗	49
date tree	zǎoshù	枣树	47
dear	qīn'ài	亲爱	48
decide	juédìng	决定	44
decision	juédìng	决定	44
deep-fried pancake	yóubǐng	油饼	43
degree	dù	度	33
delicious	hǎochī	好吃	43
delighted	yúkuài	愉快	39
department （of internal medicine, etc.）	kē	科	46
Department Store	bǎihuòdàlóu	百货大楼	36
depth of winter	lóngdōng	隆冬	33
design	shèjì	设计	47
develop	fāzhǎn	发展	36
develop （a film）	xǐ （zhàopiàn）	洗（照片）	42
diary	rìjì	日记	49
die	sǐ	死	41
direction	fāngxiàng	方向	38
director	zhǔrèn	主任	39
disappear	jué	绝	33
distant place	yuǎnfāng	远方	39
do	gàn	干	42

do business	yíngyè	营业	34
doorway	ménkǒu	门口	41
draw	huà	画	36
driver	sījī	司机	41
druggist	yàojìshì	药剂士	46
dumpling	jiǎozi	饺子	46
duration of time	shíjiān	时间	31

e

each	gè	各	43
ear	ěrduo	耳朵	43
earn	zhèng	挣	35
east	dōngbiān	东边	38
eastern part	dōngbiān	东边	38
edge （of a lake, etc.）	biān	边	44
elect	xuǎnjǔ	选举	39
elephant	xiàng	象	45
emmissary	shǐzhě	使者	45
emperor	huángdì	皇帝	41
Emperor Chongzhen	Chóngzhēn	崇桢	41
end up	liǎo	了	42
enough	gòu	够	43
enrich	fēngfù	丰富	47
enthusiastic	rèliè	热烈	40
entrance	ménkǒu	门口	41
envelope	xìnfēng	信封	34
envoy	shǐzhě	使者	45
errect	lì	立	33
even	lián...yě...	连...也...	49
every	gè	各	43
examine by fluoroscope	tòushì	透视	32
examination	kǎoshì	考试	35
exceedingly	jíle	...极了	40
except	chúle...yǐwài	除了...以外	47
excited	jīdòng	激动	40
exercise （oneself）	yùndòng	运动	40
exhausting	xīnkǔ	辛苦	31
expensive	guì	贵	44
explain	jiǎngjiě	讲解	47
explain （text, etc.）	jiǎng	讲	38

extend	jiē	接	47
extremely	jíle	…极了	40
eye	yǎnjing	眼睛	49

f

fall ill	dé（bìng）	得（病）	32
fat	pàng	胖	37
fat	féi	肥	37
fear	pà	怕	33
feel	juéde	觉得	33
feel anxiously	zháojí	著急	35
feel embarrassed	bù hǎoyìsi	不好意思	39
feel embarrassing（to do something）	bù hǎoyìsi	不好意思	39
feel tired	lèi	累	43
feeling	gǎnxiǎng	感想	47
festival	jié	节	48
festival	jiérì	节日	48
figures（in plays/novels）	rénwù	人物	44
fill	tián	填	32
fine（weather）	qíng	晴	33
finish	wán	完	39
finish	wánchéng	完成	42
fircracker	bàozhú	爆竹	48
first	xiān	先	32
fit	héshì	合适	37
flag	qízi	旗子	40
fog	wù	雾	33
folk music（for traditional instruments）	mínyuè	民乐	49
food	liángshí	粮食	48
foot	jiǎo	脚	41
for	yīnwèi	因为	48
for	duì	对	39
force	bī	逼	32
forecast	yùbào	预报	33
foreign country	wàiguó	外国	45
forever	yǒngyuǎn	永远	39
form	biǎo	表	32
form	dān	单	34
formalities	shǒuxù	手续	31

former residence	gùjū	故居	47
foster	péiyǎng	培养	47
Fragrance Hill （park）	Xiāng Shān	香山	33
fried cake	zhágāo	炸糕	43
full name	xìngmíng	姓名	34
funny	kěxiào	可笑	45

g

gardens	yuánlín	园林	44
get	ná	拿	32
get off （bus, etc.）	xià	下	38
gift	lǐwù	礼物	48
give an injection	dǎ（zhēn）	打（针）	46
give change	zhǎo（qián）	找（钱）	36
go home to visit one's family	tànqīn	探亲	44
go out	chū	出	31
go （to a place）	wǎng	往	38
goods	huò	货	36
graduate	bìyè	毕业	44
grain	liángshí	粮食	48
grandpa	yéye	爷爷	42
grass	cǎo	草	44
great	wěidà	伟大	32
Great Hall of the People	Rénmín Dàhuìtáng	人民大会堂	42
Great Wall	Chángchēng	长城	32
green	qīng	青	44
green light	lüdēng	绿灯	43
grey	huī	灰	37
grow	zhòng	种	46
gruel	zhōu	粥	43
guest	kèren	客人	39
guide	jiǎngjiěyuán	讲解员	47
guide	xiàngdǎo	向导	41

h

habit	xíguàn	习惯	33
hair （on human head）	tóufa	头发	32
hand	shǒu	手	46
hang	diào	吊	41

hang	guà	挂	34
happy	yúkuài	愉快	39
Happy New Year	gōnghèxīnxǐ	恭贺新禧	48
hard	xīnkǔ	辛苦	31
hare	tùzi	兔子	48
have a check-up	jiǎnchá	检查	32
have a fever	fāshāo	发烧	46
have a holiday/vocation	fàng（jià）	放（假）	35
have a reunion	tuánjù	团聚	48
have an injection	dǎ（zhēn）	打（针）	46
have something made	dìngzuò	定作	37
head	tóu	头	45
head（of a department）	zhǔrèn	主任	39
heart	xīn	心	32
heaven	tián	天	44
heavy	zhòng	重	42
height/build	gèzi	个子	32
heritage	yíchǎn	遗产	47
hill	shān	山	41
history	lìshǐ	历史	36
hold a meeting	kāihuì	开会	31
holiday	jiérì	节日	48
hope（as noun & verb）	xīwàng	希望	31
horse	mǎ	马	38
hospital	yīyuàn	医院	46
hot	rè	热	33
hotel	lǚguǎn	旅馆	41
hour	xiǎoshí	小时	31
how	duōme	多么	44
how	zěnme	怎么	38
human excrement	dàbiàn	大便	46
hundred	bǎi	百	33
hungry	è	饿	43

i

ice-lolly	bīnggùnr	冰棍儿	42
ice-sucker	bīnggùnr	冰棍儿	42
identical	yíyàng	一样	37
ill	bìng	病	32
illness	bìng	病	32

I'm sorry	duìbuqǐ	对不起	41
immediately	lìkè	立刻	46
Imperial Palace	gùgōng	故宫	41
improve	tígāo	提高	36
in a low voice	xiǎoshēng	小声	46
in loud voice	dàshēng	大声	34
in the past	yǐqián	以前	32
in whispers	xiǎoshēng	小声	46
increase	tígāo	提高	36
injection	zhēn	针	46
intelligent	cōngming	聪明	39
intersection	lùkǒu	路口	38
international	guójì	国际	31
it	tā	它	44
it doesn't matter	méiguānxi	没关系	41
it is said that	tīngshuō	听说	41
item	jiémù	节目	49

j

jade	yù	玉	36
job	huór	活儿	42
jujube tree	zǎoshù	枣树	47
jump	tiào	跳	44
just	cái	才	41
just	gāng	刚	38

k

keep	bǎochí	保持	40
kill	shā	杀	49
kilogram	gōngjīn	公斤	42
kind	qīnqiè	亲切	43
kind/sort	zhǒng	种	36
knock （at a door）	qiāo	敲	33
knowledge	zhīshì	知识	32
Kunming Lake	Kūnmíng Hú	昆明湖	44

l

labor	láodòng	劳动	49
lake	hú	湖	44

lamp	dēng	灯	48
landscape	fēngjǐng	风景	44
landscape garden	yuánlín	园林	44
lane	hútòng	胡同	38
language	yǔyán	语言	31
lantern	dēng	灯	48
lantern	dēnglóng	灯笼	48
Lantern Festival	dēngjié	灯节	48
Lantern Festival	Yuánxiāo Jié	元宵节	48
last	zuìhòu	最后	50
last (time)	shàng (cì)	上（次）	37
lately	zuìjìn	最近	32
later	hòulái	后来	45
lay (the table)	bǎi	摆	48
leaf	yèzi	叶子	33
lean	shòu	瘦	37
least	zuì	最	33
leave hospital	chūyuàn	出院	47
leave a message	liúyán	留言	47
leave one's comments	liúyán	留言	47
leg	tuǐ	腿	45
lend	jiè	借	49
length	chángduǎn	长短	37
let off (firecrackers)	fàng (bàozhú)	放（爆竹）	48
letter box	xìnxiāng	信箱	34
liberate	jiěfàng	解放	36
lid	gàir	盖儿	42
lie	tǎng	躺	36
life	shēngmìng	生命	32
life	shēnghuó	生活	47
light	dēng	灯	48
light (bright)	liàng	亮	43
like this	zhèyàng	这样	32
line of verse	jù	句	39
line up	páiduì	排队	38
lion	shīzi	狮子	42
list	dān	单	34
live	huó	活	47
live	shēnghuó	生活	47
liver	gān	肝	32
living	huó	活	47

local flavor/style	fēngwèi	风味	43
long	cháng	长	31
Long Corridor	Cháng Láng	长廊	44
Longgevity Hill	Wànshòu Shān	万寿山	44
look out	dāngxīn	当心	43
looks	yàngzi	样子	45
loose-fitting	féi	肥	37
lose	diū	丢	41
loudly (read, speak, etc.)	dàshēng	大声	34
love	ài	爱	45
lovely	kě'ài	可爱	45

m

mail	jì	寄	34
mail box	xìnxiāng	信箱	34
make (dumplings)	bāo	包	48
make it convenient	fāngbiàn	方便	42
make money	zhèng	挣	35
make up one's mind	juédìng	决定	44
make use of	lìyòng	利用	35
man	nánzǐ	男子	40
man of letters	wénxuéjiā	文学家	47
manner	yàngzi	样子	45
manufacture	shēngchǎn	生产	36
marble pillar (ornamental column in front of palaces)	huábiǎo	华表	42
mass	qúnzhòng	群众	47
master worker	shīfu	师傅	43
material	liàozi	料子	37
maternal grandmother	lǎolao	姥姥	46
may	kěnéng	可能	46
meaning	yìsi	意思	39
measure	liáng	量	32
medical department	nèikē	内科	32
medicine	yào	药	46
menu	càidān	菜单	43
meter (a measure word)	mǐ	米	37
middle	zhōngjiān	中间	42
midwinter	lóngdōng	隆冬	33
milk	niúnǎi	牛奶	43

mirror	jìngzi	镜子	44
mist	wù	雾	33
mistake	cuòwù	错误	47
model	diǎnxíng	典型	42
modernization	xiàndàihuà	现代化	31
money	qián	钱	35
"Monkey Creates Havoc in Heaven"	Dànàotiāngōng	大闹天宫	32
Monument to the People	Rénmín Yīngxióng Jìniànbēi	人民英雄纪念碑	42
most	zuì	最	33
motorcycle	mótuōchē	摩托车	41
mother	mǔqin	母亲	44
mountain	shān	山	41
mouth	zuǐ	嘴	32
move	bān	搬	42
move	dòng	动	42
move	gǎndòng	感动	49
moving	gǎndòng	感动	49
Museum of Chinese History	Zhōngguó Lìshǐ Bówùguǎn	中国历史博物馆	42

n

National Art Gallery	Zhōngguó Měishù Guǎn	中国美术馆	50
native	běn	本	34
near	jìn	近	44
neat	zhěngqí	整齐	48
needle	zhēn	针	46
neighbor	línjū	邻居	39
new term begins	kāixué	开学	35
New Year	xīnnián	新年	48
New Year (or Spring Festival) picture	niánhuàr	年画儿	48
New Year's Eve	chúxī	除夕	48
New Year's Eve dinner	niányèfàn	年夜饭	48
New Year scrolls	chūnlián	春联	39
next (week)	xià (xīngqī)	下（星期）	37
nice & cold	liángkuài	凉快	33
nice & warm	nuǎnhuo	暖和	33
no sooner than	yī...jiù...	一…就…	39

normal	zhèngcháng	正常	32
north	běibiān	北边	47
northen part	běibiān	北边	47
nose	bízi	鼻子	32
not only... but also	búdàn...érqiě	不但...而且...	49
not...until	cái	才	41
notebook	běnzi	本子	39
novel	xiǎoshuō	小说	41
nurse	hùshì	护士	46

O

office	bàngōngshì	办公室	42
old	lǎo	老	31
old steed in the stable still aspires to gallop a thousand li; (fig.) old people may still cherish high aspirations	lǎojìfúlì zhìzàiqiānlǐ	老骥伏枥 志在千里	39
one of...	...zhiyi	...之一	49
one's own	běn	本	34
only	cái	才	41
only	zhǐ	只	36
only	zhǐyǒu	只有	44
only a short while ago	gāng	刚	38
open	dǎkāi	打开	50
opportunity	jīhuì	机会	35
or	yàobù	要不	37
or else	yàobù	要不	37
orchid	lánhuā	兰花	50
order	dìngzuò	定作	37
ordinary mail	píngxìn	平信	34
other	biéde	别的	43
other people	biérén	别人	36
others	biérén	别人	36
outside	miànr	面儿	37
overcast sky	yītiān	阴天	33
overseas Chinese	huáqiáo	华侨	31
ox	niú	牛	47

P

pacel	bāoguǒ	包裹	39
page	yè	页	50
pagoda	tǎ	塔	44
pain	téng	疼	46
painting	huàr	画儿	36
panda	xióngmāo	熊猫	45
panda exhibition hall	xióngmāoguǎn	熊猫馆	45
park	gōngyuán	公园	33
parking lot （for bicycles）	cúnchēchù	存车处	43
pass away	shìshì	逝世	50
pass by	guò	过	41
passport	hùzhào	护照	31
paste	tiē	贴	48
patient	bìngrén	病人	46
pavilion	tíngzi	亭子	41
pay （money）	jiāo	交	37
pay a New year call	bàinián	拜年	48
pea gruel	wǎndòuzhōu	豌豆粥	43
people	qúnzhòng	群众	47
perform	yǎn	演	49
perform	yǎnchū	演出	49
performance	yǎnchū	演出	49
performer	yǎnyuán	演员	49
pharmacist	yàojìshì	药剂士	46
photograph	túpiàn	图片	34
physical examination	jiǎnchá	检查	32
picture	huàr	画儿	36
picture	túpiàn	图片	34
place	dìfang	地方	32
place （as verb）	fàng	放	34
place （a measure word）	míng	名	40
plant （as verb）	zhòng	种	46
plate	páizi	牌子	34
platform	zhǔxítái	主席台	40
play （e.g. in movies）	yǎn	演	49
play （string instruments）	lā	拉	31
player （in sports）	yùndòngyuán	运动员	40
pleasantly cool	liángkuai	凉快	33
plum blossom	méihuá	梅花	33
plump	pàng	胖	37
pneumonia	fèiyán	肺炎	32

poem	shī	诗	33
poetry	shī	诗	33
point at/to	zhǐ	指	34
point of time	shíjiān	时间	31
porcelain	cíqì	瓷器	36
possible	kěnéng	可能	46
post	jì	寄	34
post office	yóujú	邮局	34
post-office box	xìnxiāng	信箱	34
postcard	míngxìnpiàn	明信片	34
pot (a measure word)	hú	壶	36
precious	zhēnguì	珍贵	45
premier	zǒnglǐ	总理	50
Premier Zhou	Zhōu Zǒnglǐ	周总理	50
prescription	yàofāng	药方	46
present	lǐwù	礼物	48
previous (occasion)	shàng (cì)	上（次）	37
price	jiàqián	价钱	36
probable	kěnéng	可能	46
produce	shēngchǎn	生产	36
programme	jiémù	节目	49
public	gōnggòng	公共	38
push	tuī	推	43
put	bǎi	摆	48
put	fàng	放	34
put forward	tí	提	43
put in order	shōushi	收拾	48
put on a show	yǎnchū	演出	49
put somebody to trouble	máfan	麻烦	48
put up	guà	挂	34

q

quality	zhìliàng	质量	36
quite	bǐjiào	比较	43

r

rabbit	tùzi	兔子	48
radio	shōuyīnjī	收音机	48
radio (/wire-broadcasting) announcer	guǎngbōyuán	广播员	41

rain	yǔ	雨	33
rain（as verb）	xià（yǔ）	下（雨）	33
raincoat	yǔyī	雨衣	37
realize	shíxiàn	实现	31
receipt	shōujù	收据	34
receive	shōu	收	34
recently	zuìjìn	最近	32
record	jìlù	记录	40
record	lùyīn	录音	46
recording	lùyīn	录音	46
recover	huīfù	恢复	47
red autumnal leaves	hóngyè	红叶	33
red lotus	hónglián	红莲	50
rediculous	kěxiào	可笑	45
refreshments	xiǎochī	小吃	43
regard as	zuò	作	47
register（a letter, etc）	guàhào	挂号	34
register card	guàhàozhèng	挂号证	46
regular	zhèngcháng	正常	32
relieve oneself	jiě	解	46
remain	liú	留	39
remember	jì	记	39
repair	xiū	修	38
respectively	gè	各	43
restaurant	fànguǎn	饭馆	43
result	chéngjī	成绩	35
retain	bǎochí	保持	40
retire	tuìxiū	退休	39
reunite	tuánjù	团聚	48
rich	fēngfù	丰富	47
ride（a bycicle）	qí	骑	37
right	zhèngquè	正确	49
road	lù	路	31
road	mǎlù	马路	38
rock	shí（tou）	石（头）	42
rostrum	zhǔxítái	主席台	40
ruin the effect by adding what is superfluous（fig）	huàshétiānzú	画蛇添足	36
ruler	chǐ	尺	42
run	pǎo	跑	37

sack	dài	袋	48
same	yíyàng	一样	37
scenery	fēngjǐng	风景	44
school	xuéxiào	学校	31
school begins	kāixué	开学	35
sea	hǎi	海	50
seat	zuòwèi	座位	38
second (a measure word)	miǎo	秒	40
see (a doctor)	kàn (bìng)	看（病）	35
sell	mài	卖	49
semester	xuéqī	学期	35
sentence	jù	句	39
serious	lìhai	厉害	46
serve	fúwù	服务	43
set (a meassure word)	tào	套	36
shadowbox	dǎ (quán)	打（拳）	40
Shanghai	Shànghǎi	上海	31
shop	diàn	店	43
shop assistant	shòuhuòyuán	售货员	36
shop assistant	yíngyèyuán	营业员	34
shopkeeper	zhǎngguì	掌柜	49
short	duǎn	短	37
short note	tiáozi	条子	39
short story	xiǎoshuō	小说	41
shout	hǎn	喊	44
show	yǎnchū	演出	49
shut	guān	关	46
side	biān	边	44
sign	jì	迹	33
sign	páizi	牌子	34
silk fabric	chóuzi	绸（子）	37
simple & unadorned	jiǎnpǔ	简朴	47
situation	qíngkuàng	情况	35
sky	tiān	天	44
slip of paper	tiáozi	条子	39
smile	wēixiào	微笑	50
snack	xiǎochī	小吃	43
snack bar	xiǎochīdiàn	小吃店	43
snow	xuě	雪	33

so	suǒyǐ	所以	44
so	zhème	这么	42
so	zhèyàng	这样	32
socialism	shèhuìzhǔyì	社会主义	31
society	shèhuì	社会	49
socks	wàzi	袜子	37
solo	dúchàng	独唱	43
some	yǒude	有的	34
son	érzi	儿子	48
soprano	nǚgāoyīn	女高音	49
sore	téng	疼	46
south	nánbiān	南边	38
South Asia	Nán Yà	南亚	45
southern part	nānbiān	南边	38
spectator	guānzhòng	观众	40
speak	jiǎng	讲	38
specialized subject	zhuānyè	专业	35
specialty	zhuānyè	专业	35
spend one's holidays	dùjià	度假	44
spoken drama	huàjù	话剧	49
sport	yùndòng	运动	40
sports meet	yùdònghuì	运动会	40
sportsground	cāochǎng	操场	40
sportsman	yùndòngyuán	运动员	40
spring	chūntiān	春天	39
Spring Festival	chūnjié	春节	48
Spring Festival couplets	chūnlián	春联	39
squad	bān	班	42
square	guǎngchǎng	广场	41
square meter	píngfāngmǐ	平方米	42
squeeze	jǐ	挤	41
stamp	yóupiào	邮票	34
stand	lì	立	33
stand erect/upright	tǐnglì	挺立	50
state of affairs	qíngkuàng	情况	35
statue	gèzi	个子	32
stockings	wàzi	袜子	37
stomach	wèi	胃	32
stone	shí（tou）	石（头）	42
stool	dàbiàn	大便	46
stop（said of bus, etc.）	zhàn	站	38

store	diàn	店	43
story	gùshi	故事	38
stout	pàng	胖	37
street	mǎlù	马路	38
street	jiē	街	39
strange	qíguài	奇怪	35
subscribe to	dìng	订	36
subway	dìtiě	地铁	38
succeed	chénggōng	成功	49
such	zhème	这么	42
such	zhèyàng	这样	32
sufficient	gòu	够	43
sugar	táng	糖	43
suggest	tí	提	43
Summer Palace	Yíhéyuán	颐和园	33
summer vocation	shǔjià	暑假	35
sun	tàiyáng	太阳	44
sunglasses	mòjìng	墨镜	45
surprised	qíguài	奇怪	35
surrender	qūfú	屈服	33
sweep	sǎo	扫	48
sweet dumplings made of glutinous rice flour	yuánxiāo	元宵	43
synopsis	shuōmíngshū	说明书	49

t

tablet（a measure word）	piàn	片	46
tail	wěiba	尾巴	47
take	ná	拿	32
take （along）	dài	带	38
take away	bān	搬	42
take care	dāngxīn	当心	43
take somebody as	zuò	作	47
take X-ray examination	tòushì	透视	32
talk	huà	话	31
tall	gāo	高	37
Tangshan	Tángshān	唐山	36
tasty	hǎochī	好吃	43
taxi	chūzūqìchē	出租汽车	38
tea service/set	chájù	茶具	36

teacup	cháwǎn	茶碗	36
teahouse	cháguǎn	茶馆	19
teapot	cháhú	茶壶	36
telegram	diànbào	电报	34
tell	jiǎng	讲	38
ten thousand	wàn	万	42
term	xuéqī	学期	35
terminal point	zhōngdiǎn	终点	38
terminus	zhōngdiǎn	终点	38
terrible	lìhai	厉害	46
test (as verb)	kǎo	考	35
test	kǎoshì	考试	35
theatre	jùchǎng	剧场	49
there is no need to	búyòng	不用	31
there is something wrong with	huài	坏	49
therefore	suǒyǐ	所以	44
they (for things/animals)	tāmen	它们	44
thick	hòu	厚	36
thin	shòu	瘦	37
thin	báo	薄	34
thing	dōngxi	东西	30
think	juéde	觉得	33
think of	huáiniàn	怀念	47
thirsty	kě	渴	43
this	běn	本	34
though	suīrán	虽然	39
thoughtful	zhōudào	周到	41
thousand	qiān	千	42
Tian'anmen (Gate of Heavenly Peace)	Tiān'ānmén	天安门	34
Tian'anmen Square	Tiān'ānmén Guǎngchǎng	天安门广场	41
ticket office	shòupiàochù	售票处	41
ticket seller	shòupiàoyuán	售票员	38
tidy	zhěngqí	整齐	48
tidy up	shōushi	收拾	48
tiger	lǎohǔ	老虎	47
tight	shòu	瘦	37
time (a measure word)	cì	次	31
to	duì	对	39

to the highest/lowest degree	zuì	最	33
touch （one's feeling）	gǎndòng	感动	49
toward	wàng	往	33
trace	jī	迹	33
track	jī	迹	33
trade	màoyì	贸易	44
traditional Chinese calendar	xiàlì	夏历	48
traffic light/signal	hónglǜdēng	红绿灯	38
travel	lǚxíng	旅行	44
tree	shù	树	33
troublesome	máfan	麻烦	48
turn a corner	guǎiwān	拐弯	38
turn into	chéng	成	47
type/kind	zhǒng	种	36
typical	diǎnxíng	典型	42

u

uncle	dàye	大爷	38
uncle （father's younger brother）	shūshu	叔叔	39
under	xiàbiān	下边	34
underground	dìtiě	地铁	38
underneath	xiàbiān	下边	34
United States of America	měiguó	美国	31
university	dàxué	大学	31

v

vacation	jiàqī	假期	35
valuable	zhēnguì	珍贵	45
vanish	jué	绝	33
various	gè	各	43
verse	shī	诗	33
violin	xiǎotíqín	小提琴	31
visitor	kèren	客人	39
visitors' book	liúyánbù	留言簿	47

w

wall	qiáng	墙	34
ward （of a hospital）	bìngfáng	病房	46

wardrobe	yīguì	衣柜	39
warm	nuǎnhuo	暖和	33
warm	rèliè	热烈	40
wash	xǐ	洗	41
way	lù	路	31
we	zánmen	咱们	38
wear (cap/glasses/gloves)	dài	戴	45
weather	tiānqì	天气	31
welcome	huānyíng	欢迎	38
west	xībian	西边	41
western part	xībian	西边	41
Wester-style suit	xīzhuāng	西装	37
what	duōme	多么	44
whole	quán	全	48
why	zěnme	怎么	38
why	wèishénme	为什么	34
wide	kuān	宽	42
wind	fēng	风	33
window	chuānghu	窗户	44
window	chuāngkǒu	窗口	34
winter jasmine	yíngchūnhuā	迎春花	50
winter vocation	hánjià	寒假	35
wish (as noun & verb)	xīwàng	希望	31
wish somebody a happy New Year	bàinián	拜年	48
with much toil	xīnkǔ	辛苦	31
woollen sweater	máoyī	毛衣	37
words	huà	话	31
work	gàn	干	42
work	láodòng	劳动	49
work	huór	活儿	42
works (of literature/art)	zuòpǐn	作品	49
workshop	chējiān	车间	39
world	shìjiè	世界	50
wrap	bāo	包	48
wrist watch	biǎo	表	35
writer	wénxuéjiā	文学家	47
writings	wénzhāng	文章	47
wrong	chuò	错	38

y

| yield | qūfú | 屈服 | 33 |
| youth | qīngnián | 青年 | 47 |

z

zero	líng	零	36
Zhou Enlai	ZhōuĒnlái	周恩来	50
zoo	dòngwùyuán	动物园	45

Appendix III

(Stroke Number)

Character	Pinyin	Character	Pinyin
2		办	bàn
了	liǎo	艺	yì
3		**5**	
之	zhī	立	lì
下	xià	市	shì
山	shān	它	tā
才	cái	玉	yù
千	qiān	本	běn
马	mǎ	古	gǔ
干	gàn	布	bù
广	guǎng	只	zhǐ
4		叫	jiào
天	tiān	出	chū
片	piàn	生	shēng
分	fēn	包	bāo
牛	niú	句	jù
尺	chǐ	北	běi
手	shǒu	片	piàn
比	bǐ	石	shí
公	gōng	平	píng
毛	máo	世	shì
内	nèi	打	dǎ
方	fāng	主	zhǔ
司	sī	永	yǒng
已	yǐ	东	dōng
元	yuán	厉	lì
长	cháng	礼	lǐ
风	fēng	边	biān
订	dìng	发	fā
专	zhuān	节	jié
历	lì	圣	shèng
		叶	yè
		兰	lán
		让	ràng

记 jì

6

交 jiāo
米 mǐ
次 cì
死 sǐ
百 bǎi
成 chéng
考 kǎo
地 de
老 lǎo
灰 huī
吊 diào
丢 diū
竹 zhú
年 nián
先 xiān
血 xuè
各 gè
全 quán
收 shǒu
耳 ěr
合 hé
决 jué
冰 bīng
存 cún
江 jiāng
自 zǐ
西 xǐ
因 yīn
页 yè
亚 yà
刚 gāng
扫 sǎo
动 dòng
毕 bì
设 shè
伟 wěi
价 jià

灯 dēng
机 jī
讲 jiǎng
向 xiàng
阴 yīn
阳 yáng
杀 shā
众 zhòng
华 huá
过 guò
当 dǎng
爷 yé
关 guǎn
观 guān

7

彷 páng
完 wán
冷 lěng
初 chū
抓 zhuā
把 bǎ
作 zuò
肝 gǎn
改 gǎi
但 dàn
豆 dǒu
利 lì
李 lǐ
社 shè
汽 qì
希 xǐ
辛 xìn
杏 xíng
尾 wěi
针 zhēn
连 lián
邻 lín
坏 huài
邮 yóu

- 162 -

话(huà) 建(jiàn) 终(zhǒng)

9

洗(xǐ) 活(huó) 首(shǒu) 美(měi) 度(dù) 亮(liàng) 封(fēng) 挣(zhèng) 指(zhǐ) 厚(hòu) 胃(wèi) 秒(miǎo) 重(zhòng) 科(kē) 胖(pàng) 拜(bài) 保(bǎo) 便(biàn) 查(chá) 春(chūn) 咳(ké) 恢(huī) 胡(hú) 南(nán) 故(gù) 皇(huáng) 亭(tíng) 兔(tù) 炸(zhá) 修(xiū) 珍(zhēn) 带(dài) 挂(guà) 贴(tiē) 绝(jué)

劳(láo) 枣(zǎo) 块(kuài) 运(yùn) 怀(huái) 护(hù) 体(tǐ) 近(jìn)

8

所(suǒ) 使(shǐ) 放(fàng) 雨(yǔ) 表(biǎo) 青(qīng) 枝(zhǐ) 拉(lā) 往(wǎng) 肥(féi) 爬(pá) 怕(pà) 阿(ā) 拐(guǎi) 阜(fù) 肺(fèi) 刮(guā) 屈(qū) 昆(kūn) 周(zhōu) 油(yóu) 奇(qí) 叔(shǔ) 货(huò) 侨(qiáo) 实(shí) 卖(mài) 医(yī) 单(dān) 诗(shì)

壶预绸养热样桥钱顾饿透逝宽

hú yù chōu yǎng rè yàng qiáo qián gù è tòu shì kuān

11

得寄雪接推累船袋第够脚彩假梅麻培设探野眼黄换瓷盖辆

dé jì xuě jiē tuī lèi chuán dài dì gòu jiǎo cǎi jià méi má péi shè tàn yě yǎn huáng huàn cí gài liàng

种奖树独骆钢选挤虽柜药钟觉临铰脏迹退草

zhòng jiǎng shù dú luò gāng xuǎn jǐ suī guì yào zhōng jué lín jiǎo zàng jì tuì cǎo

10

座站记病疼被高海班套株借拿航料凉旅唐除

zuò zhàn jì bìng téng bèi gāo hǎi bān tào zhū jiè ná háng liào liáng lǚ táng chú

碗零路跳暖微群错颐雾摆简　wǎn líng lù tiào nuǎn wēi qún cuò yí wù bǎi jiǎn

14

襄演敲鼻腿旗熊瘦　guǒ yǎn qiāo bí tuǐ qí xióng shòu

15

篇躺摩鞋摹墨薄聪　piān tǎng mó xié mó mò báo cōng

16

糖嘴操激镜　táng zuǐ cāo jī jìng

绩骑检菜惯　jī qí jiǎn cài guàn

12

湖渴著提晴短象最量跑幅喊街粥景寒隆牌舒痛暑掌愉棉逼遍缎遗塔　hú kě zhe tí qíng duǎn xiàng zuì liáng pǎo fú hǎn jiē zhōu jǐng hán lóng pái shū tòng shǔ zhǎng yú mián bǐ biàn duàn yí tǎ

13

填搬　tián bān

18　　　　　　　dài

戴

19　　　　　　bào

爆